Empower
Yourself

J. P. Vaswani

Published by:

GITA PUBLISHING HOUSE
Sadhu Vaswani Mission,
10, Sadhu Vaswani Path,
Pune - 411 001, (India).
gph@sadhuvaswani.org

EMPOWER YOURSELF
©2014, J. P. Vaswani

ISBN: 9789380743615

DADA VASWANI'S BOOKS
Visit us online to purchase books on self-improvement, spiritual
advancement, meditation and philosophy.
Plus audio cassettes, CDs, DVDs, monthly journals and books in Hindi.
www.dadavaswanisbooks.org

Printed by:
MEHTA OFFSET PVT. LTD.
Mehta House,
A-16, Naraina Industrial Area II,
New Delhi - 110 028. (India).
info@mehtaoffset.com

Empower
Yourself

J. P. Vaswani

Gita Publishing House,
PUNE, (India).
www.dadavaswanisbooks.org

Books and Booklets by Dada J.P. Vaswani

7 Commandments of the Bhagavad Gita

10 Commandments of a Successful Marriage

100 Stories You Will Never Forget

108 Pearls of Practical Wisdom

108 Simple Prayers of a Simple Man

108 Thoughts on Success

114 Thoughts on Love

A Little Book of Life

A Little Book of Wisdom

A Simple and Easy Way To God

A Treasure of Quotes

Around The Camp Fire

Be An Achiever

Be In The Drivers Seat

Begin the Day with God

Bhagavad Gita in a Nutshell

Burn Anger Before Anger Burns You

Comrades of God - Lives of Saints from East & West

Daily Appointment with God

Daily Inspiration (A Thought For Every Day Of The Year)

Daily Inspiration

Destination Happiness

Dewdrops of Love

Does God Have Favorites

Finding Peace of Mind

Formula for Prosperity

Friends Forever

Gateways to Heaven

God In Quest of Man

Good Parenting

Highway To Happiness

How to Overcome Depression

I am a Sindhi

I Luv U, God!

In 2012 All Will Be Well!

Joy Peace Pills

Kill Fear Before Fear Kills You

Ladder of *Abhyasa*

Lessons Life Has Taught Me

Life after Death

Life and Teachings of Sadhu Vaswani

Life and Teachings of the Sikh Gurus

Living in the Now

Management Moment by Moment

Mantras For Peace Of Mind

Many Paths: One Goal

Many Scriptures: One Wisdom

Nearer, My God, To Thee!

New Education Can Make the World New

Peace or Perish: There Is No Other Choice

Positive Power of Thanksgiving

Questions Answered

Saints For You and Me

Saints With A Difference

Say No to Negatives

Secrets of Health And Happiness

Shake Hands With Life

Short Sketches of Saints Known & Unknown

Sketches of Saints Known & Unknown

Stop Complaining: Start Thanking!

Swallow Irritation Before Irritation Swallows You

Teachers are Sculptors

The Goal Of Life and How To Attain It

The Little Book of Freedom from Stress

The Little Book of Prayer

The Little Book of Service

The Little Book of Success

The Little Book of Yoga

The Magic of Forgiveness

The Miracle of Forgiving

The New Age Diet: Vegetarianism for You and Me

The Perfect Relationship: Guru and Disciple

The Terror Within

The Way of *Abhyasa* (How To Meditate)

Thus Have I Been Taught

Tips For Teenagers

What You Would Like To Know About *Karma?*

What You Would Like To know About Hinduism?

What To Do When Difficulties Strike?

Why Do Good People Suffer?

You Are Not Alone: God Is With You!

You Can Change Your Life

Why Be Sad?

Preface

You are the architect of your own destiny!

Your life, your dreams, your future, your destiny are in your own safe hands. To shape your life and your destiny, all you need to do is to empower yourself to bring about the positive transformation you seek.

God endowed each and every one of us with a free will, and each of us has the freedom to change our destiny at every step, in every round of life. At every step of life, we can make the effort to improve our condition. Through our actions, we can actually succeed in changing our own karma and thus change our own destiny.

Is this not true empowerment?

"As a man thinketh, so he becomes," is the immutable law of human nature. Fill your mind with thoughts of joy, love, peace and harmony – these aspects will be reflected in your life.

Today in the modern world, we all lead "extremely busy lives". "There's no time!" is the repeated refrain we hear all around us.

But then, we don't seem to have any time for ourselves! Can I ask you how many of you meditate daily? Can I ask you how many of you sit in a silence corner and recite your favourite *shloka* or *mantra* daily? Can I ask you how many of you take time out to go for a walk?

Let us empower ourselves to make our lives more beautiful, more peaceful, more serene, more fulfilling! Let us cultivate greater awareness, so that we live in the present, and enjoy everything that we do – whether it is drinking tea, washing dishes, drawing up strategy, planning a project, cooking, walking, talking or just sitting quietly.

True, human life is full of pain and suffering. But equally, it is also filled with many wonders and joys. Sunshine, laughter, music, the green grass, the company of our friends, the presence of our loved one – the list is endless.

If we are not happy, if we are not at peace with ourselves, we cannot share peace and joy with those around us. It is only when we begin to radiate peace and joy, that we spread positive vibrations around us.

Discover the secret of inner joy and peace that no one can take away from you. Empower yourself and be a conductor of joy and peace to everyone around you!

Index

Chapter 1
What kind of Story are you Living?

There's a book called 'A Million Miles in a Thousand Years' about an author who is being interviewed to make a movie about his life. And he realises his life is boring. There is almost nothing worth talking about. In writing the screen play and editing the book events into interesting movie dialogue, Miller learns a little more about the elements of a good story and through those things learns more about the story that he is living as well as the story he wants to be living. "Good stories don't happen by accident, I learned. They are planned." he says in the book.

My friends, let us ask ourselves, "What kind of story am I living? What kind of story do I want to be living?"

An Iranian king summoned a philosopher and said to him, "I would like you to sum up human life in a few simple words."

"Just give me a week's time," requested the philosopher. The week passed by quickly. The philosopher returned to the king's court, "I have thought over your question carefully," he said "I believe I have the answer now." "Give it to me at once" pleaded the king eagerly. "The lives of most people can be summed up in these few words, O king," said the philosopher. "He was born, he grew up in years, he married, he begot children, he died!"

Is this going to be my story? Is this all there is to human life? These words also sum up the life of every animal. Is not a human being's life meant for higher things?

Have you ever asked yourself, "What is the purpose of my life?" Have you ever thought, "I race and I chase, all so that I can make more money, have more success, become more powerful, acquire more and more. All this chasing for what?" We stride through life as if we will live forever. We treat time as a cheap commodity that we blindly waste. And before we know it, the sands of our hourglass run out, and we face the end of our brief existence on this planet unfulfilled and regretful.

Little do we realise that the human birth has been given to us for a specific purpose. We are like the astronaut on a Space Shuttle Mission sent to explore life on Mars. We are given vital supplies and are equipped with the latest hi-tech gadgetry. However, we are so fascinated by the beauty and splendor around that we forget our real purpose, which was to report our findings back to earth. Similarly in life, we are busy doing so many things, we are so wrapped up in worldly pursuits that we have forgotten our true purpose. We have forgotten why we are here because we have forgotten who we are.

Man is a combination of three things, the physical body, the mind and the soul. Most of us, have identified ourselves as the body that we wear. If I were to ask you who are you, you would immediately point to your body. We think we are the bodies that we wear. But the body, as has been told us in the great scripture of India, the Bhagwad Gita, is only a garment which we have worn during our present incarnation. We have worn many such bodies. We have put away many such bodies. We are not the bodies which we wear. Neither are we the body-mind complex. Man is essentially a soul who has worn the garment of the body and who has brought with himself the instrument of the mind to be able to do his work on the physical plain. Each one of us is an immortal spirit.

My friend, this priceless human birth has been bestowed upon each one of us for a specific purpose – that we may realise what we are, whence we came, and whither we are to return. We are not the bodies that we wear. We are immortal spirits. We are not this; we are That! Weapons cannot cleave us and fires cannot burn us, and winds cannot dry us and the waters cannot drench us. We are that, we are not this.

We have received the golden opportunity of the human birth, let us not leave the world with empty hearts. While all of us need to work and earn our livelihood, we must not forget our true purpose, we must not neglect the Treasure Imperishable, the treasure of true love. Let us fill our hearts with Love - love for the Lord and love for his suffering children. It is to gather this treasure that we have come to this earth. Alas, how few of us realise the value of human life! How many of us fritter away this precious gift in trivial pursuits!

Chapter 2
Take Care of your Moments

Time is the most precious gift that God gives us during our earthly life. Most of us just fritter it away, unmindful of the fact that we can never reclaim even one second that we throw away! Every morning you are handed 24 golden hours - 1440 precious minutes. Every one of us is given the same number of hours every day. Rich people cannot buy more hours. Scientists cannot invent more minutes. Misers cannot save time to hoard it and spend it another day. If you had all the money in the world, you couldn't buy an extra minute. And yet, it has been pointed out, time is always fair and forgiving. No matter how much time you have wasted in the past, you have a full day before you every morning. What will you do with this priceless treasure?

Once a management teacher wanted to teach his students about the importance of prioritising time. He brought a big jar with a wide mouth and some materials in a bag. First he put into the jar about a dozen small rocks. They filled up the jar. He asked the students, "Is there more space?" unanimously the students replied, "No!"

From the bag he removed some loose gravel and poured it into the jar. It filled up the spaces in between. He shook the jar and as it settled to the bottom, he filled some more.

He asked the students again, "Is there room for more?" They replied in many voices, "Maybe," "It's possible."

The professor poured into the jar some fine sand. He shook the jar and poured some more. He then poured into the jar some water. He then asked his students, "What do you think is the purpose of this illustration?" One student quickly replied, "No matter how busy your schedule is, if you try very hard you can always fit in more."

The professor shook his head. "The real purpose of this illustration is to understand that if you don't put the big rocks in first then you can never get them in at all." What do the big rocks signify? They signify things that make your life-story meaningful - time with the family, prayer and communion with God, spending your time for a worthy cause and helping others whose need is greater than ours.

The professor concluded, "Find time for the Purpose of Life, the rest is all pebbles and sand."

In this busy modern world it has become all too easy to let time, the most valuable possession of life, slip away from us. E-mails, internet, multiple television channels, cell phones and all the other products of the technological revolution that were supposed to have simplified and enhanced the quality of our lives seem to have conspired to strip us of the time needed for the really important things of life.

Remember, priorities are not what you say they are—they're what you actually do. So take a moment to reflect on how you spend your time, what your priorities have been lately, until now. And reflect on whether those are the priorities you want to live. If not, let's look at how to change the situation—as simply as possible. What are some of the important things that should occupy our time?

Friends, there are many important things, which we need to do in life. Sadly enough we keep postponing them. One such thing is our appointment with God. We find time for everything else in the world, but we forget the one thing needful, our daily appointment with God. The mind which is always preoccupied with mundane affairs, keeps prompting us to attend to this or that activity; thus we check our mail every fifteen minutes; we talk on our mobile phones even when we are driving; we listen to music as we commute to work; we 'grab' a sandwich or take a coffee break even while we are working on the computer. We are ever so busy making money and adding to our bank balance. But we neglect our credit account in the Bank of Providence. We spare no thought for the life hereafter. Even as you allow time for all other activities, allow time for the most important of all tasks - your daily appointment with God.

Every day, preferably at the same time and the same place, go and sit in silence, pray, meditate, do your spiritual thinking. The secret of a successful, rewarding, satisfying life is to overcome the dull and distracted states of the mind - and reach the highest state of consciousness - a state in which the mind is not only one-pointed but absolutely mastered.

Life is very short and every minute we have must be well utilised so that we can make something worthwhile of our life. Gurudev Sadhu Vaswani, said to us again and again: "Time is the most precious of all possessions, therefore take care of your minutes, and take care of your moments." Every moment is valuable; we don't realise the value of time until the last moment comes. It is then that we say, Ah! What did we do?

Chapter 3
Empower Yourself

I well remember how one day a man came to Gurudev Sadhu Vaswani and said to him, 'I am an utter failure. I have suffered a nervous breakdown. I am suffering from an internal incurable disease. I have lost my job, my house is sold out, my furniture and belongings are mortgaged. My friends and relatives have deserted me, I have lost everything in life.' And to him Gurudev Sadhu Vaswani said, 'You say that you have lost everything. You have not lost everything, you have but lost the things that come and go, you have but lost the things, which the world gives, and the world takes away. Within you is the power that can heal any internal disease. And within you is the treasure that can deliver you from any financial crisis.

Within you is a tremendous power. Trust it and though the heavens fall yet it will deliver you, it can never fail in delivering you.'

Within every one of us is the power of our greater self, but we are unaware of it. We spend so much of our energy telling ourselves we are not doing good enough, we have very little time and energy left to look inside and discover our true potential. Our condition is very much like a lion in a cage. When the lion was first locked up within a cage he struggled to be free. He wanted to break the bars for then he was full of energy, he was full of zest, he was full of vigor, he was full of strength. He struggled to be free, he tried to break the bars, but the bars were too strong for him. His energy was dissipated. He felt exhausted. And he settled down to live in the cage like any other small helpless creature. In due course he forgot that he was a lion. This is our condition too. We have forgotten what we are, we have forgotten our higher self, our true self in which is hid this infinite power of the spirit. We have forgotten it and we have identified ourselves with the cage. We have identified ourselves with the body. This is our great tragedy. To live an empowered life, we must break the cage and become conscious of our greater self.

There is a beautiful story told us in the ancient books, of a king's son. He is only 3 years old when the king decides to send him away to a far off city. The father wants the prince, to rub shoulders with the common man so that he may be acquainted with their struggles and their strivings, so that he may know the troubles and tribulations through which they have to pass. A nurse is put in charge of a prince who takes him to a far off city. There he studies in a school. He grows in years, he has finished his education. And now he is asked to earn his own livelihood. He has to face the struggles of life, he earns his livelihood to pay for his food, to pay for his lodging, to pay for his other expenses. He comes in contact with some friends, who take him to the night club. There he experiences the excitement of life in night clubs, he gambles, he drinks he has affairs with many girls. Gradually he becomes a habitual gambler. Almost every day he returns home very late at night and now he appears to be frustrated with life, this life which is sunk in pleasure.

One night he returns very late, there he sits outside the door of his house out in the cold, in his hands is a knife. He is about to pierce it in his chest when the nurse who is watching him from the window quietly opens the door, comes and meets him and says to him, 'You are late again.' And this man says, 'Yes I am late again, I did not wish to disturb you at this late hour.' And after sometime the young man adds, 'I am frustrated with life. I find that life has no meaning. I find that life has no significance why should I not end this life?'

Then it is that this nurse places her hands on his shoulders, she looks straight into his eyes and says to him, 'If only you knew who you are, you would not be the man that you have become.' And in sheer astonishment this young man asks, 'Who am I?' And the nurse says to him, 'You are the future king of our country.' 'A king! How may that be?' And the nurse reveals to him his true identity. When he hears that, the royal element within him is awakened. He goes to the woods and lives there in solitude for a week. When he returns, he says to the nurse, 'I want to go to my father and thank him for having given me this wonderful experience.' It was a bright sunny day when the father and the son, when the king and the prince met together on the steps of the palace amidst rejoicing and music.

Every one of you is a prince, every one of you is a son of the king, the king of the universe. You have forgotten this and therefore you feel frustrated again and again, you feel depressed and dejected. You are not aware of your true self for you are enclosed within a shell of ignorance. Break the shell and you too will know. You too will experience the life of a prince, a life of freedom and fulfillment.

Chapter 4
Be What You Truly Are

Human beings have a natural tendency to conceal all their misdeeds. We try to cover them with falsehood, pretense and hypocrisy. The reason for this is of course, our big 'Ego'. We tend to wear many masks, some masks are painted bright and some masks are pure and glowing. But most of us know that they are only masks, the fake camouflage that we put on. We present to the world, an unsullied, pure and beautiful exterior faked to please others. These masks of falsehood can deceive the world, but not oneself. And in the long run, if we continue to play 'roles' under these fake exteriors, it can cause harm to both our physical and emotional health. Is there anyone among us who can say that he has not sinned? Is there anyone who can frankly say that he has harboured no ill feelings or ill thoughts towards others?

One day, a saint along with his disciples was passing by a graveyard. It was a moonlit night. The very graves shone with the silvery light of the moon. The saint looked at the graveyard, and remarked, "Man is like those graves! See, they appear shining and clean from the outside, but when you dig the graves deeper, you will find nothing but a sordid collection of insects and worms, feeding on dead flesh!

In the same way, man may appear very clean from outside, but look deeper into him, you will find venomous snakes of greed, serpents of evil thoughts and wasps of desires. Man goes about wearing white clothes, man goes about putting on a white exterior, but man's heart is filled with the slush of evil. His mind is full of lust and greed and unhealthy desires!"

Looking at the graveyard, the saint urged his disciples, "Do not carry the dead spirit within. Come out of the graves, and live a life of reality! Do not hide your sins. Do not conceal your crimes and evil doings; do not keep them under wraps. Be natural. Be what you truly are. Not the dead bodies of the graveyard, but the zestful, joyful human beings of the beautiful planet earth!"

Once, Gurudev Sadhu Vaswani was asked, "Please show us an easy way to realise the Higher Self. We are unable to follow the difficult paths described in the scriptures." He replied, "I will show you the easiest way. By morning you would have realised your Higher Self."

The devotees surrounding him were happy. Self-realisation in one night! Anyone of them would have thought it was impossible. But here Gurudev Sadhu Vaswani was offering us self-realisation on a golden platter.

He said, "Tonight, you must keep awake; take a sheet of paper, and write on it all the sins that you have committed till now. Tomorrow, early in the morning, you must go and put it up on the notice board outside the Mission Office. Once you have put up the list of all your sins of commission and omission on the notice board of the Mission you will find your Higher Self."

The eager devotees were bewildered. Thoughtful and serious, they retired for the night – perhaps, to keep a vigil!

Next morning everyone rushed to the notice board. Alas, there was not a single sheet of paper confessing anyone's sins and misdeeds. No one was ready to reveal the inner sullied self. Finding the Higher Self could wait!

Friends, we are content to live our lives on the surface. Superficiality characterises everything we do. We occupy our minds with what we would like to eat, what we would like to buy, and what we could do to impress our friends and neighbours. Do not put up a show for the sake of the ego. Do not be like a fake currency note.

You will be rejected not only in the temple of the Lord, but also in the world around you. Be genuine. Follow the truth. Accept your shortcomings, your sins and your faults. Do not hide your weaknesses. Be an open book in the court of the great dispenser of justice. You will be able to cross the bar and withstand the test of time only if you are 'real'. Understand this clearly: you cannot hide your true self from God.

Therefore pray again and again, "Oh Lord, make my heart pure, wash it whiter than snow, cleanse me of all this filth, all this dirt."

Chapter 5
Move On and
Start A New Chapter

What is done is done. What is gone is gone. One of life's lessons is always moving on. Moving on doesn't mean you forget about things, it just means you accept what happens and continue living happily.

A couple was going to visit a friend. They waited for a bus at the bus stop. Suddenly the husband realised that his wallet was missing. The wallet contained probably a good amount of money and naturally he was upset. He tried to look into all his pockets. He was quite sure he put it in his left pocket when he left home, but where is it gone? He called his son at home and asked him to check his drawers to confirm he had not left it there. He even re-traced a few steps to see whether the wallet had accidently dropped down. But the wallet was nowhere to be found. Dejected and disheartened, he stood there wondering what to do. The bus which he had to board came by, he wouldn't get into the bus. Another bus came, he wouldn't get into that bus either. A third bus came and he wouldn't get into the bus until his wife said to him, "Are we going to sit and cry here all the time or are we going to go on? Are we going to be here worrying about the lost wallet or are we going to move on?"

This is a lesson that each one of us has to learn. There are so many situations and circumstances in life that are not to our liking. But, how long can we allow ourselves to wallow in sorrow and self-pity? The call of life is Onward, Forward, Godward! close the door to the past, open the door to future, take a deep breath, step on through and start a new chapter in your life.

A very dear one passes away, suddenly he is snatched away from us, how long will we keep on weeping about it?

There was a woman who came to me and said, "Three months ago I lost my husband and I have been weeping, shedding tears day and night." And she said to me, "I am not exaggerating but I tell you literally during these three months I must have wept at least three buckets of tears." Three buckets of tears, just imagine! I said to her, "You have wept three buckets of tears, has your husband come back?" She said, "How can my husband come back. They took him to the cremation ground, they burnt the body, all we got was a little ash, that is all." Then I said, "What is the use of shedding all those tears? Why don't you put your feelings to some useful purpose?"

Her husband was a leader of his community and I told her, "There are so many things that you must be knowing about him that are not known to the people, why don't you sit and write your reminiscences." She liked the idea and started doing that. She came to me after a year, on the first anniversary of her husband, she had that book published. And her face was wreathed in smiles. She said, it is a wonderful suggestion that you gave me, and I feel so happy, ever since I have followed it.

True acceptance in the right spirit is a dynamic concept which encourages us to do our very best, to put forth our best efforts to achieve what we desire. But, if we cannot achieve those results, you must accept it as the Will of God, in the knowledge that there must be some good in it. As I always say, there is a meaning of mercy in all the incidents and accidents of life.

I remember how one day Gurudev Sadhu Vaswani visited Manney's Bookshop. As we were looking at the new arrivals, I came across a book, entitled, 'My Philosophy'.

So I took this book to him and said, "This is a new arrival, may be you will be interested in it. This book contains philosophies of many great ones, but tell me what is your philosophy?" He answered, "My philosophy!

The philosophy of acceptance, I know of nothing higher. Nothing outer can hurt you for the universe is not merely just, the universe is essentially good. The cosmic soul is love and humanity is his bride."

In one of his books, Joel Osteen says, "You

must make a decision that you are going to move on. It won't happen automatically. You will have to rise up and say, 'I don't care how hard this is, I don't care how disappointed I am, I'm not going to let this get the best of me. I'm moving on with my life."

Chapter 6
Shift Your Focus

Your life is a manifestation of the thoughts that go on in your head. Your life is a mirror of dominant thoughts that you think. Your mind thinks thoughts and the pictures are broadcast back as your life experience. You can change your life by changing the pattern of your thinking. If you want to change things, change the channel and change the frequency of your thoughts.

There was a professor of economics who was discussing the theory of demand and supply with his students. At the end of the session, he asked the students, "Can you name anything, any product or service of which the supply always exceeds the demand?"

Even before the others could apply their minds to the question, one student shot up like an arrow and said, "Sir, I can tell you one thing of which the supply always exceeds the demand. That thing is 'PROBLEMS'. Their supply is unlimited, even when our demand for them is NIL."

He was right. Wasn't he? The pathways of our life seem to be strewn with problems and challenges. There is hardly a day when we don't handle some problem or the other. It is as if they are waiting in a never-ending queue outside your door; barely have you handled one problem when another immediately rears its head. Getting caught up in a problem isn't just frustrating it can literally stress you out. Focusing on the problem rarely helps matters. Instead, it only wastes your time and energy as you go over it repeatedly in your mind. Instead of dwelling on the problem, get your mind off it. Shift your focus. Step away from the issues and turn your attention to the Lord. He will automatically free us from our worries, and take care of all our 'concerns' and 'problems'.

I remember when I was a school boy; a holy man visited the town in which I lived. And I was very fond of meeting holy men. I used to go and sit at their feet, get their blessings, listen to their teachings. And when I took leave of this holy man, I said to him, "Please, give me a teaching."

Do you know what he said to me? And the teaching that he gave me was in a few simple words. He said, *"Sher bano kuta nahin bano."* - Be a lion, do not be a dog.

I was thoroughly bewildered. I couldn't understand the meaning of those words. I told him hesitatingly, "Sir, I am a lion already because I am born in the sign Leo, but what do you mean by saying, be a lion do not be a dog?"

The holy man explained, "You may have seen if you throw a ball at a dog, the dog will run after the ball, but if you throw anything at the lion, fire a bullet at him, he will not care for the bullet, he will not care for the ball, he will come and take hold of you. He goes to the thrower, not to the thrown."

We are all the time thinking of that which has been thrown to us, we think of circumstances and conditions of life, the changing vicissitudes of life, the changing phenomenon, the passing shows of life. We do not think of Him, the Thrower, who has thrown all these things at us! We do not concentrate on Him from whom it has come, the giver, the Thrower who has thrown all these things at us!

I read an anonymous statement which said: Focus on God who puts you in touch with the Infinite so that your mind can grapple with the finite successfully. Therefore, empty your mind of all worry and anxiety. Renounce everything; throw out everything; don't think of anything but meditate on Him; concentrate on Him; think of Him; dedicate all your work to Him. Shift your focus from the problem to the Lord! Resting your mind in the Divine Presence, as it were, focuses the mind, energizes and vitalises your intellectual abilities so that you are able to give your best to the situation at hand.

Problems do not come to us by accident. They are deliberately thrown in our way by a beneficent Providence for our own good. Instead of worrying about them, let us turn to God in prayer and place all our burdens at His Lotus Feet. This will give us an immediate feeling of peace and relaxation, enabling us to tackle the problems and perplexities of life in a spirit of calm surrender.

Remind yourself, again and again, of the beautiful lines "O heart, why do you worry? So what if difficulties have come your way, the remover of difficulties is not far away."

Chapter 7
Play Your Part Well

Why do we often feel upset, frustrated, disappointed? Because we are attached, because we are involved. When we expect others to satisfy our desires, and they disappoint us, as they inevitably must, we experience distress. And this distress takes the form of anger, frustration, disappointment and depression. If I do my work, if I live my life as if I am playing a part, I would not be upset. All the world's a stage, and all the men and women merely players, they have their exits and their entrances; said Shakespeare.

If something happens in a play, do you feel troubled? Supposing another 'character' in the play shouts at you or speaks ill of you, do you get angry? No! You know in the heart within that it is just an act and you have to play your part well. If you don't play your part well the entire drama will be spoiled.

I remember, when I was a little boy scout, we had a variety entertainment show. And in this show, I was made to play the part of Napoleon, the great emperor. There I stood in my imperial majesty. In a succeeding scene I was given the part of *Taatiya*. I was supposed to be a boy servant to a *zamindar*. Now, this *Zamindar*, this landowner was one of my common soldiers when I played the part of Napoleon. Now, this landowner tells me fiercely, '*Taatiya*, bring me a glass of water'. I felt tempted to tell him, 'What do you mean! Five minutes ago I was the great emperor Napoleon, you were one of my common soldiers. How dare you tell me to bring you a glass of water?' But I'm happy I did not yield, I did not succumb to the temptation. Otherwise, the whole drama would have been spoiled.

You have to play your part well. That is all you're required to do. What affects us is the sense of attachment. I get attached to an individual. Now that individual drops me out and I feel disappointed, I feel sad. We have to get over this attachment. Therefore, life gives us such experiences so that we grow in the spirit of detachment. Man has come to this earth plane to become a master man and you cannot become a master until you grow in the spirit of detachment. Therefore, always regard yourself as an actor on the stage of life, playing your part to the best of your ability.

A famous actor once remarked, "In a particular film, I was made to play the role of the husband of a woman whom I disliked strongly. I would not like to see her face at all but in that film I had to play the role of her husband and I played it very well. I showed that woman that I loved her immensely and she was the only one whom I cared for in the whole world. But that was only for so long as we were facing the camera. When we got out of the studio, I would not even look at her or speak to her."

Each one of us has a role to play in the great cosmic drama of life. This drama is unfolding itself day by day. But, of course, there's a catch. In the cosmic drama of life, you have to play a double role. You have to be an actor and you also have to be a spectator. You have to watch the play unfolding before your eyes and you also have to act. If you are able to do this well, you will not lose your peace of mind. Why is it that we lose our peace of mind? Because our wishes, our desires, are crossed. We want a particular thing to be done in a particular manner.

When it happens in a different way, perhaps in exactly the opposite way, our peace is lost. If only we can realise this, that we are all actors in the drama of life; that the role we are playing have been given to us by the Cosmic Director we will never feel distressed.

It is not easy to do this maintain your inner equilibrium at all times and in all situations. Gurudev Sadhu Vaswani used to tell us, "God upsets our plans to set up His own. And His plans are always perfect." If I have the faith that whatever has happened to me is according to the plan of the Highest, that there is some hidden good in it for me, I will not be upset.

Once you realise this, there is no more frustration, no more unhappiness. You abide in a state of tranquility and peace. You may not be able to achieve this straight away. It is a process through which you must move.

Chapter 8
Empty your Cup

Many of us think we are free, that we have a choice in all we do. But in reality we are not free. We are 'bound' to our desires and cravings. You may not like it when I tell you that you are a prisoner of yourself. Let me ask you to do a little introspection. Ask yourself whether you are truly free from all desires, ambitions, wishes and cravings. You will have to admit the truth, that you are a slave of your desires and dreams. If you are 'caged' by your own desires, if you are a 'prisoner' of your own passions, then how can you consider yourself free? How can you be happy? How can you enjoy the bliss which is your birthright?

There is an ancient story that a king wanted to grant a particular holy man a wish. He asked the holy man what he would like as a gift, and the holy man said he would like the king to fill his cup with gold coins. The king thought that this would be a very easy way to please the holy man, but when he tried to fill the cup, it just would not fill. No matter how much money the king put into it, it would still not fill the cup.

In frustration the king asked the holy man to tell him the secret of the cup, and the holy man replied: "This cup is like the heart of every man, which is never content. Fill it with whatever you may, with wealth, with greatness, with power, with knowledge, with all there is. It will never fill. It is not meant to be filled."

Not knowing this secret, man goes on in pursuit of every object continually, and the more he gets, the more he wants, the cup of his desires is never filled. It is said that the worldly desires are like the salty waters of the sea. Such waters can never quench man's thirst. On the contrary, his thirst increases and his craving for fresh water grows even more acute! To drown yourself wholly in this worldly life is akin to quenching your thirst with salt water.

Desires are of many types: and all desires must go before we can enter into a life of freedom and joy. "Cut down the whole forest of desire," urged the Buddha, "not just one tree only!" And a great mystical writer of our days has expressed the same thought very beautifully in words which I cannot forget, "A man who has been killed by one enemy is just as dead as one who has been killed by a whole army."

If you are a slave to one desire, you are as spiritually dead as another who is a victim to a hundred desires. You may be a man of many virtues, but if you are held down by just one desire, you are as a cup of milk with a single drop of poison in it: the entire milk is poisoned.

The question was asked of a sage, what is it that distinguishes a human being from a brute beast? What is the difference between the two? Both of them belong to what they call the animal kingdom, and yet man is different from an animal, from a beast, what is it that distinguishes one from the other? And the Sage answered: "What distinguishes man from the brute beast is self control. The animal cannot control himself. He is a creature of his instincts. But man has been given this gift. If he so desires, he can control his cravings, his animal appetites, his passions, his lust, his greed, his hatred. Man is meant to be a master of passions not to be mastered by passions. He is meant to be a master but so many of us alas are no better than slaves. We are slaves of our own desires, our own cravings our own animal appetites."

Human beings are constantly swept and tossed by the storm of desires. We are all subjects of the mind. The mind wants to rule. Therefore Gurudev Sadhu Vaswani urged us to make friends with the mind. He explained that the mind binds us to the world but it can also liberate us. Therefore, do not fight the mind but make it your powerful ally.

The mind binds us by creating needs and desires in our hearts. However, if the mind gives up desires, if it gives up all wants, one can become a free soul. So let us befriend the mind.

The mind wants to concern itself with the

pleasures of the senses but let us train it to go within and seek the One. 'Seek the One, and you will find the All.'

Chapter 9
Don't Chase Happiness...
Create it

Supposing you were told, 'Today is the last day of your life. Make a list of all the things that you feel you have accomplished, all the things that have made you feel truly happy; what are the things you would put down in that list, knowing that you have only hours left to live?'

I'm certain that your car, bungalow and bank account will find no place on the list. What you are sure to put on it would be the most fundamental elements of a truly happy life — your love for God, the love and respect you have earned from your near and dear ones, the sunshine you brought into people's lives by your warmth and affection, the compassion you have received from your friends, the love and kindness you have shown to people. Happiness is in the little things that make life significant.

Many of us are apt to equate happiness and success with money, material wealth and possessions. The Wise Ones remark, This is sheer ignorance. You cannot be happy just because you live in a mansion or a penthouse apartment. You cannot achieve peace and inner harmony just because you drive a Mercedes or a BMW. You cannot be considered 'successful' just because you are a millionaire.

Happiness is an *inner* quality! Don't look for happiness...create it. It was Abraham Lincoln who said, "Most are about as happy as they make up their minds to be." And since happiness gives meaning and purpose to life, we must know where to find it. All the world's greatest philosophers agree on this point: true happiness stems from within us, from a way of thinking about life. This is the most enduring, agreed upon truth about happiness: if the prints of contentment and satisfaction are not within, no material success, no pleasure or possession make us truly happy.

I recall the words of that wise man, G. H. Loruner. He worked for several years as the editor of the 'Saturday Evening Post', and on one occasion he wrote words which have clung to my memory. Loruner says, "It is good to have all the things which money can buy. But it is also good to pause for a while again and again and check whether we have not lost all the things which money cannot buy".

There are so many things which money cannot buy, and those are the things that contribute to true happiness. Money can buy for us the softest bed in the universe, but money cannot buy for us sleep. Money can buy for us medicines, but money cannot buy for us health. Money can buy for us the best cosmetics in the world, but money cannot buy for us that natural rosy tint in the cheeks. Money can buy for us the best of foods, but money cannot buy for us appetite. Money can buy for us flatterers who will follow us wherever we go, but money cannot buy for us true friendship. Money can buy for us all the books that are available in the world, but money cannot buy for us brains. Money can buy for us social prestige, but money cannot buy for us a clear conscience.

William Lyon Phelps was a distinguished writer and critic, as well as a popular Professor at Yale University. He had inspired and guided hundreds of students during his long and distinguished career. When he was asked to write a message of guidance and inspiration for the American people, he asserted: "The principle of happiness is like the principle of virtue: it should not be dependent on things, but be a part of your personality."

When Professor Phelps had been a young student, he had drawn inspiration from the words of President Timothy Dwight who had visited his college and addressed the students. Dwight had told them emphatically: "The happiest person is the person who thinks the most interesting thoughts."

This was what he taught his students too. Real happiness cannot come from external things, he told them. The only lasting happiness that you will experience is that which springs from your inner thoughts and emotions. Therefore, he urged them, cultivate your mind. For an empty mind seeks mere pleasure as a substitute for happiness. The happiest people are not the ones who make money, buy property and own stocks. The happiest people are those who cultivate their minds with interesting and invigorating thoughts.

Chapter 10
Let It Go!

L ife is full of incidents, pleasant and unpleasant. When an unpleasant thing happens, we are apt to lose our balance: this creates a negative emotion which expresses itself in a feeling of sadness, or depression. An effective way of dealing with such a situation is to go to the root of the matter and 'let go' of what is causing the negative emotion. Let it go! Let everything go!

Has my sister failed to understand me? Let it go! Has my brother spoken ill of me? Let it go! Has my best friend turned against me? Let it go! Have I suffered loss in business? Let it go! Have my plans been upset? Let it go! Have I been treated with disrespect? Let it go! Has a dear one cheated me? Let it go! Has the health of someone dear to me suffered a set-back? Let it go!

There was a gardener who loved each tree, each plant, each little shrub in his garden so dearly that he would not cast away the dead leaves and the withered branches. He stored them all in his garden.Gradually all the space in his small garden was taken up by the dead leaves and dry branches, and the beautiful garden wore the appearance of a garbage heap.

Are we not so many of us like this gardener? We go on storing worries and anxieties, failures and frustrations, fears and disappointments, which are better cast away and forgotten. And the beautiful garden of our life turns into a wasteland!

If we wish to be happy, we must unclutter our 'house'– the house of our heart. We must throw out all the joy-killers, the negative thoughts of greed, ill will, jealousy, malice and envy. But throwing these out is not enough – we must fill our minds with happy thoughts – thoughts of purity, prayer, sympathy, service and sacrifice, love and kindness, prosperity and peace, success and victory.

A troubled conscience will never allow us to live in peace and quiet - and our conscience will continue to remain troubled unless we rid ourselves of the hatred and resentment that make us unforgiving, the joy-killers that disturb our calm.

The past is over and done with. It is gone with the wind! Therefore, I say to you, release it once and for all! Let it go!

This is the best way to handle all your failures, disappointments, hurdles, and grievances - release them, let them go! We can do this simply by erasing the slate of our mind. We can refuse to think of them - and just deny their existence in our mind. You see, the only existence they have is in your mind!

There is a beautiful little incident in the life of Aesop, the great story-teller. One day, Aesop is playing with little children, shouting and laughing with them. An Athenian passes by, he expresses surprise that such a grown-up person should waste his time thus.

In answer, Aesop picks up a bow and, unstringing it, lays it on the ground. To the Athenian, he says, "O wise one, tell me the meaning of this unstrung bow!" The man is perplexed, he finds no suitable answer. "I cannot solve your riddle," he says, "tell me, what it means." Aesop says to him, "If you keep a bow always bent, it will lose its elasticity. But if you let it go slack, it will be fitter for use when you want it."

Are we not, many of us, like that bent bow, always highly strung? We need to unstring ourselves, to relax, from time to time, that we may be 'fitter for use' when we are called to action. To relax, we need to learn to 'let go'. The secret of relaxation is in three words: 'Let it go'!

If we wish to achieve inner peace, there is only one way - release ourselves from anger and resentment, learn to let it go.

Remind yourself that anger hurts you more than the person who upset you, and visualise it melting away as an act of kindness to yourself.

In this transitory world — a world in which things come and go, nothing abides — is there anything worth worrying over?

Let it go! You can't start the next chapter of

your life if you keep re-reading the last one. The more we let go, the more do we conserve our energies for the constructive and creative tasks of life.

Chapter 11
Build Faith and Find Joy

Faith is the one true source of support on which we can always rely in the rough and tough journey called life upon this earth. Faith is like Wi-Fi. It is invisible but it has the power to connect you to what you need.

There was a knock at the door, and the children trembled in fear. "Hush, my darlings!" comforted their mother, The Lord is with us, and we have nothing to fear!

It was a tough time for the family, who lived in a small New York apartment. Their father had passed away suddenly, leaving his widow to fend for herself and the three small children. He had left no savings, and the family was plunged into poverty, from their comfortable lifestyle.

The widow had very little money— but she had strong faith in the Lord. She instilled the quality of trust in her children, telling them again and again, Trust in the Lord! He will never forsake us. To earn her livelihood, she rented a sewing machine, working at night with a dim light to pay for her children's food and education. She kept the family going, as best as she could.

But now, it was the end of the month she found that she had no money left to pay for the rent of her sewing machine. Only the previous day, the rent-collector had warned her that the machine would be taken away if she did not pay the rent within 24 hours.

Here was a knock at the door! There was not a cent at home. What could the mother do? What would become of them if the sewing machine was taken away? The children trembled in fear. "God will always provide for our needs", their mother had said. Where was He now?

The mother opened the door. On the steps stood a stranger, with a baby in his arms. He spoke urgently, "Madam, I need your help very badly! My wife has fallen ill and had to be admitted to a hospital. There is no one at home to look after the baby. We have just moved into this neighbourhood, and people told us you are the right person to take care of the baby, in the absence of her mother. We will pay you $10 an hour. Will you please look after our treasure?"

The mother stretched out her hands to receive the baby. She raised her eyes to Heaven, as she said, Oh God! Wonderful are Thy ways, Thou wilt never forsake Thy own.

When you place your trust in the Lord, when you surrender utterly and completely to His Divine Will, you will find wonderful things happen in your life! Faith is the ray of sunshine that lights up the dark, deep caverns of the human heart. Faith is the beautiful, fragrant flower that blooms even in the wilderness of despair and suffering. Faith is the sustenance for all human endeavours. It is the greatest blessing that God can bestow upon us! Man does not have to climb a mountain peak, nor has he to wander in the forest, to discover the power of faith. Man can be linked with the Divine wherever he is. All he has to do, is call out to the great Almighty with faith in his heart and God responds immediately. When our bond with God is strong, we realise that God is our helper, our protector and our guardian and guide. Like Newton's Law of Gravitation, we have the Law of Faith. We gravitate towards His love, and His love does the rest. This Law works only when we surrender ourselves utterly and completely to God. And then, the experience of His greatness, His kindness and His benevolence becomes a part of our lives. Life is full of uncertainties, the unknown and the unknowable. Even when you think you've curled into a cozy cocoon of predictability, anything could change in a heartbeat. Living with uncertainty generates stress and unhappiness – and this kind of strain can be conquered by faith and devotion. Faith sees the invisible, believes the incredible and achieves the impossible.

Therefore, trust in the Lord! Faith is necessary not only in crisis situations and emergencies, but also to battle the exhausting, crushing routine of everyday life. Build faith and find joy.

There was a sister who was under

tremendous pressure both at work and on the home front. The company she worked for was passing through a financial crisis, and was severely short-staffed, with each employee doing the work of two or three people. There was no question of complaining, because she knew she was lucky to have a job, while a dozen others like her had lost theirs. At home, she had an old mother to care for and a younger brother and sister to support. Sometimes, she said, she was overwhelmed by the thought of what lay ahead for her when she awoke in the morning.

I gave her a simple prayer. Every morning, as she awoke, I told her to hand her day over to the Lord and tell Him, "Lord, this day is Thine, and all the work I do, I offer to You. I know I cannot carry the load myself. I hand my life over to You. I beg You to get everything done for me." She found a miraculous change in her life. Everything seemed to fall into place; her burdens seemed to lift of their own accord. Everything seemed, somehow, more manageable! Repose your faith in Him, and see how He is always there for you, by your side, when you need Him!

Chapter 12
Nourish the Soul

It seems that we try to pack more and more things in our daily schedule but hardly any of these nourish our soul. We care so much for our body but we pay scant attention to our souls.

A famous doctor lived in a remote part of India and carried on his work of help and healing sincerely. A certain man in this small town fell very sick and refused medical assistance.

The good doctor heard about the sick man and went to see him immediately realising the seriousness of his condition. He checked on the man and declared that he was down with a severe bout of bronchitis.

Promptly he wrote out a

prescription and gave it to the sick man. The man feebly asked, "When should I take the medicine?"

The doctor calmly answered, "You can take it after a month." The wife was aghast and quivered, "A month. He may not even be alive after a month." The doctor coolly said, "Ok, then take it after a week." To this the patient protested, "Sir, the way I am coughing, I am not sure if I can survive for a week." "Alright then", said the doctor casually, "Why not take it tomorrow." This time both of them exploded, "Doctor! Don't you realise how sick I am." Unperturbed the doctor responded, "Well then, take it now."

We are like sick people who know we are ill, but are hesitant to take the medicine that is prescribed to make us well. Yet, until we do, there will be no hope for recovery. Our souls are sick and need to be healed.

However, we busy ourselves with the myriad things of life and ignore the most important aspect of our being, our soul. Interestingly enough we don't always have to go out to look for a doctor for the soul. The saints and Holy Ones often come to our aid. They can see the gravity of our sick souls and prescribe the panacea that will resolve all our ailments, that is chanting of the Name Divine. They prescribe the medicine but we refuse to take it putting it off to a later time of our life. Alas, we do not realise that death may snatch us at any time. All our procrastination will then be of no use. We may lose this golden chance of the human birth that we have received. Let us not put off for tomorrow what we can do Now.

Chanting the Name Divine is the potent pill that can cure all ills. My friends what a wonderful thing it would be if each one of you carried but this one thought with yourself today. Even as you do your daily work, chant the Name Divine, sing the name of God, any name that appeals to your heart. It may be *Rama Krishna Hari!* It may be the *Mahamantra: Hare Rama! Hare Rama! Rama! Rama! Hare! Hare! Hare Krishna! Hare Krishna! Krishna! Krishna! Hare! Hare!* It may be the ancient word 'Om'. It may be the word that has been dear to the heart of India through ages untold '*Rama, Rama, Rama*'. It may be the name Krishna. It may be the name Jesus, it may be the name Ahura Mazda, it may be the name Allah. Any name that appeals to you for all names belong to Him, who is the Nameless One. He is Nameless, though the sages have called him by many names. Choose any Name that draws you. Repeat it again and again. Repeat it not merely with the tongue but with feeling and emotion. Repeat it with tears in your eyes. So many years have sped by, but little time remains for us. Let us utilise that time, let us make it rich and fragrant by uttering the Name Divine.

The Name of God is at once pure and purifying. It purifies those that sing it with deep love and longing of the heart. The importance of the repetition of the Holy Name as a tool to cultivate the soul has been emphasised by all the saints and sages of India. Chant the Name over and over again until the Name blends with the every breath of your being.

If I can utter incessantly the Name which is sweeter than all names – the Name of Him whose countenance is of the colour of fresh cloud, whose face is more lustrous than the full moon, whose enchanting eyes are lovelier than the lotus, whose ruby lips draw rich melody and music out of a simple reed – I need no other prayer, no spiritual discipline.

Those that sing the Name of God with every breath of their being cross over to Yonder Shore, where beauty smiles and wisdom is radiant.

Chapter 13
Connect with
the Cosmic Divine Energy

I often see my young friends rushing to 'charge' their cellphones whenever they see a spare plug point. They explain that they have been making and receiving so many calls that the charge is running out.

My dear friends, we are taxing our minds and hearts with so much useless activity all day long. Do we make any effort to recharge them? Our minds and hearts too need to be charged and recharged by contact with the greatest source of strength and vitality - God.

A young man, due to circumstances which he felt were beyond his control, found himself in a sorry plight. He was a graduate of an Indian University, but, do what he will, he lost job after job, which he secured not without much seeking and strenuous effort. He could not procure food for his famished wife and children. On top of it, he was afflicted with what the doctors called an incurable disease. He felt like one ship-wrecked; and, not unoften, he wished for death to come and grant him release from the agonies of an unfruitful existence.

One day, as he wandered aimlessly through the streets of his town, like a dead leaf borne on the autumn-wind, he happened to pass by a House of Worship. And floating on the breeze there came to him the words of a song:

Arise! Awake! O child of God!
Thou art not a slave of circumstances:
Thou art the master of thy destiny!
Come out of the slough of depression
And behold!
The very planets are eager to serve thee!

He paused for a while to listen to the song: was the song being sung for him? Word after word sank deep into his heart. And, irresistibly, he felt drawn to the open door; he entered the big hall and took his seat in a corner. Soon the song came to a close, it was followed by *kirtan*, brothers and sisters singing together in chorus a few simple words:

> O Friend of the friendless and forlorn!
> O Lord of the lowly and lost!
> I cast my cares at Thy Lotus-feet!
> I seek refuge in Thee!

The lines were sung, again and again, in religious fervour. Our friend, too, joined in the singing. And as the pitch of the song rose, he forgot himself, his trials and woes, his sorrows and suffering, and for the first time, in several years, he knew what it was to feel happy.

Friends, *kirtan* is spiritually elevating! When continued for a long time, it spreads its beautiful, peaceful vibrations and uplifts the soul! Evening after evening, he came to join in the worship and the *kirtan*. It gave a new tone to his life. Gradually, his life underwent a transformation. The pattern of his mind was changed; his thoughts became positive, vital. His health improved. He became a new man. And, today, this young man, no longer young in years, for he is over fifty, is at the head of a big commercial firm with God as his "Senior Partner". More than half of the profits, they run into six figures, he sets apart for the service of God and his suffering creation.

We are, most of us, victims to the machinations of our mind. The mind sits over us as a tyrant and we readily consent to be its slave. So many of our ills would be cured, if only we could change the pattern of our mind. Change the mind and you change the world. Perhaps, the simplest and most efficacious method of correcting our thinking is that of *kirtan*. Whenever two or three gather together, let them sing in chorus the Name Divine and in the Name lose themselves, drown themselves. This method is so simple that often its importance is overlooked. But it is one of immense value to us all.

Chanting the Name Divine, cleanses us of all 'interior' dirt and ugliness. It takes away the negativity that is deep within us. *Kirtan* helps us to bond with the Cosmic Divine Energy. It attracts Divine Light, because praising the Lord, singing His glories is a way of acknowledging His Presence. As you practice staying connected, you will feel energy flowing through your body often manifesting in a flow of peace as well as a flow of inspired ideas.

Just as we clean our body with soap and water, similarly we can purify our mind and heart by washing them in the waters of the spirit, the *amrit dhara* of *kirtan*, that flows perennially in the *satsang*. Do not ever forsake this beautiful, purifying, blissful experience, that is so freely available to all of us. It is as easy as walking in and taking your seat. The power of the *satsang* will take care of the rest.

Chapter 14
Put your little hands into God's great hand

A great and wealthy man once said that of all the experiences of life he treasured one incident that gave him unmixed joy of the sort he had never felt.

As he came out of his bank in Mumbai and was about to signal his chauffeur a little girl came up to him, looked into his face and put her tiny hand into his great one and said, "Sir, I am frightened of the traffic. Will you kindly take me across the street to the other side?"

Relating this incident the man said, "It was a great honour for me to take the trusting child across to the other side. It taught me that when I find myself in a difficult position, all I have to do is to put my little hand into God's great hand. He would be as delighted as I was to take this little child to the other side."

Are you passing through a dark night when not a single star doth shine? Do you suffer from a disease which the doctors have declared as incurable? Are you on the verge of a financial crisis, on the verge of bankruptcy with no one to help you out?

Are you involved in a personal relationship problem which in spite of your best efforts you are unable to solve? Hand over the problem to the Lord - hand it over in child-like trust. Say to him, "You are my father my caring father, you are my sweet mother. I cannot handle this problem by myself. Can you handle it for me? For me this has become impossible. For you it is possible." Hand it over. Put your little hand in the Lords great hand.

But the condition is that once you have handed over the problem, you don't have to think of it again. If you think of it again and again, then God says I will stand aside, you go and handle your problem yourself. You must not think about it.

But this you will find very difficult to do as the mind has formed the habit of turning round and round, around our problems. The mind will drag you to the problem even though you may not want to do it, the mind will drag you to the problem again and again. It is at those times that you should utter some affirmation which may give you strength to face the mind. An affirmation like:

Tum bina meri kaun khabar lay
Govardhan Girdhari or
Jis ke sir upar Tu mera Swami
so dukh kaisay pavah or

The Lord is my shepherd; I shall not want

Keep on repeating it again and again. It is not to be uttered once, but you must repeat it again and again. It is like sending out shots from your pistol at the mind. The mind will be subdued.

Tum bina meri kaun khabar lay
Govardhan Girdhari
Tum bina meri kaun khabar lay
Govardhan Girdhari

These affirmations, whether they are spoken loudly or whether they are uttered silently in the heart within, are equally effective. You can pick up any affirmation that appeals to you. Keep on repeating it again and again. This is very necessary. As you keep on repeating it over and over again you will be able to subdue the mind.

One of Oliver Cromwell's officer's was given to the habit of constant anxiety and worry. His faithful servant was a pious man who wished to help his worrisome master. The servant said to him, "Master, is it not true that the Lord ran this world long before you came into it?" "Sure" said the master, "He did." And the servant asked again, "You believe that He will run it after you have left, don't you?"

Again the master nodded assent. "In this case," said the servant, "why don't you stop worrying and let Him run the world while you are in it?" The servant was a man who knew what it was to cast his cares upon the Lord.

The man of faith, the man who has put his little hand in the great hand of the Lord, is like a rock in the midst of an ocean, waves come and strike the rock, the rock is unmoved. A holy man lay on his deathbed as his end drew near. Some of his devoted disciples began to sob bitterly. But the holy man continued to smile. "It matters little whether one lives or dies," he said. "If I die I shall be with God; if I live God will be with me."

Compassion is the litmus test of spirituality on Earth. Rituals do not constitute religion. Singing *bhajans* and clapping hands is not religion. These are but outward forms of expression. The essence of religion is spirituality. And spirituality is best expressed through compassion.

In a pretty, little story, we read that the Angels asked God if there was anything in the world stronger than rocks.

"Yes," answered God, "stronger than rocks is iron; for iron can break rock."

" Anything stronger than iron?" asked the Angels.

And the Lord answered, "Fire; for iron may be melted in fire."

"Anything stronger than Fire?"

asked the Angels.

And the Lord said, "Yes, water; for fire is quenched by water."

"Anything stronger than water?" the Angels asked again.

And the Lord answered, "Yes, wind; for wind may scatter water."

"Anything stronger than wind?" asked the Angels.

"Yes," said the Lord, "sympathy is stronger. And nothing there be that is stronger than the compassionate heart."

Compassion, *maitri*, will be the key to the new social order.

Today, our hearts have become hard as stones. But once our hearts are lit with devotion and love, the hard crust falls off. When the heart is filled with love it becomes soft, it acquires the capacity to sympathise and empathise with those in sorrow and suffering and with those in distress.

I would describe compassion as the crown of all virtues. I believe it is this quality that takes us closest to the Divine within each one of us. When we practise — not just feel — compassion, when we go out of ourselves to reach out to others and alleviate their suffering, we rise to the Highest Self in us. Need I say that at such times, negative feelings of strife and disharmony are totally nullified in our hearts and minds? And when more and more of us practise the divine quality of compassion, will our world not move towards lasting peace?

Compassion is the root of religion! Because compassion brings with it kindness, it brings love, it brings fellowship, and it brings service. A man whose heart is filled with compassion is a friend of all, he is kind and loving to all. Such a man is kind not only to human beings but even to birds, animals and insects.

Here is a beautiful but simple definition of compassion that a friend shared with me: 'Compassion is the humane quality of understanding the suffering of others and wanting to do something about it.'

Albert Schweitzer was always pained to hear people say, "If only I were rich, I would do great things to help and serve others." He would promptly point out to them that all of us could be rich in love, generosity and compassion; and that we could always extend our loving care and compassion to others. This, he said, was worth more than all the money in the world!

All of us have something to give! Let us give what we can to others our time, our talent and know-how, our effort, our understanding, our love, our concern, our sympathy, our smiles. Let us give with love and compassion. Even if one person is comforted by your words; even if one person's broken heart is healed by your understanding; even if someone's misery is wiped out by your kindness – you have made a difference!

Can you read? Then read to a blind student. Can you write? Then write a letter, fill a form for someone who is not as lucky as you are. If you are not very hungry, share your food with someone who is. If you are at peace with yourself, reach out to those who are in pain, and disturbed by their suffering.

The distinguished American author and lecturer, Leo Buscaglia, once talked about a contest he was asked to judge. The purpose of the contest was to find the most caring child. The winner was a four-year-old child whose next-door neighbour was an elderly gentleman who had recently lost his wife. Upon seeing the man cry, the little boy went into the old gentleman's yard, climbed onto his lap, and just sat there. When his mother asked him what he had said to the neighbour, the little boy said, "Nothing, I just helped him cry."

As the Dalai Lama says, "If you want others to be happy, practice compassion. If you want to be happy, practice compassion."

Chapter 16
Switch on the Sunlight

Have you ever passed through a gloomy period of your life— a dark night when not a single star doth shine? Then switch on the sunlight! This can be done through prayer— by turning to God. Let us turn to him again and again, discuss with him our plans and programs, our trials and tribulations and ask him to help us in furthering them. God is the one friend of all friends. He is our one unfailing companion; he is our comrade in life and death. Let our day be full of little turnings to the Lord.

Out of prayer floweth peace. Within each one of us is a fountain of joy and peace. We touch the fountain through prayer and drinking its waters, slake our thirst and are refreshed, revitalised. The man of prayer is at peace with everyone and in all conditions. His heart is ever anchored to the One.

Keep on shooting small, brief prayers to Him all the time. But you will say to me, "We live in a world of stress and strain. We do not even have time to pause for a breath, where do we have the time for shooting prayers?" You do have the time, even you who are so busy, even you have the time. Perhaps, you have dialed a number. You want to speak to somebody on the phone. The bell is ringing. Until someone comes and picks up the telephone on the other side, you have some little time. Why don't you use it in shooting a brief prayer? 'God I am going to speak to so and so now, so bless our conversation that it may be of mutual benefit.' How long did it take? Perhaps, a few seconds; that you would otherwise fritter in useless thoughts.

You are driving in the car or waiting for a bus to arrive to take you to the office. Instead of letting your mind wander in circles why not spend that time in having what I call divine romances with God. We can have divine romances with God any time. Converse with Him, say to him, "I love you God. I want to love you more and more. I want to love you more than anything in the world. I want to love you to distraction, to intoxication." Or in the evening, you have to attend a party. You are ready but your spouse is not ready. Instead of fretting and fuming in the heart within, why not engage yourself in a loving conversation with God? You have the opportunity to do so. You should feel grateful to your spouse for being late in getting ready.

It was Brother Lawrence who said, "There is not in the world a kind of life more sweet and delightful that that of a continual conversation with God." Grow in the constant awareness of God's presence. Keep on shooting brief prayers all the time. The idea is that even as the needle of the compass always points to the north, even so the needle of your heart should always point to God.

May I give you one simple personal experience? I was standing at a bus stop. And there I found a man, I did not know him. I had never met him. I had never spoken to him. But I found that he was sad. He was dejected. He looked depressed. So I just shot a prayer at him. I said, "God, he is also your child. He appears to be so sad and dejected. Why don't you bring sunshine into his heart? Let his face smile." And after a while I found that there was a soft smile on his lips. I don't know what made the difference. But keep on shooting these brief prayers all the time.

What a great mercy of God that we have him with us all the time, all the 24 hours of the day and night. We can turn to him at any time of the day or night without having to previously fix an appointment with him. And we can share with him our inner most secrets without the least hesitation. Others might laugh at our crude ways, they might scoff at our childish attitudes but to God we can speak any thing for he loves each one of us even as a mother loves her only child. And love is always patient, always forgiving, always understanding, always trusting and true.

In this dark and desolate world of *Kaliyuga*, it is only our contact with God that can offer us support and protection. If one takes the sun with him, he can find no shadow. As soon as the sun turns on a shadow, the shadow darkness disappears. The same is true of life; if one takes God with him, who is the Spirit of Light, the darkness of sorrows and troubles of life disappear. Blessed is he who makes

God the centre of his life, turning to Him, again and again, as the one abiding presence. His life is rooted in prayer and he works wonders, unseen even by his intimate friends.

Chapter 17
Walk ye the Little Way

In today's competitive environment, humility and gentleness are apt to be taken as signs of weakness, rather than goodness! We feel that if we are humble and meek, people will treat us as doormats and walk all over us. But the truly successful people are the ones who are humble and modest.

It was a wise man who reminded us, "It is well to remember that the entire population of the universe, with one trifling exception, is composed of others." People who are genuinely humble, know that the 'others' are significant; they know that many of these 'others' can be pretty intelligent and pretty interesting. They know that there is a lot they can learn from other people; therefore, they treat everyone with respect and courtesy.

In his seminal work 'Good to Great: Why Some Companies Make the Leap...And Others Don't', Jim Collins mentions humility as a crucial quality for leadership. In this book, Collins examined companies that went from good to great by sustaining 15-year cumulative stock returns. Among the many characteristics that distinguished these companies from others is that they all had a Level 5 leader. Level 5 leaders direct their ego away from themselves to the larger goal of leading their company to greatness. These leaders are a complex, paradoxical mix of intense professional will and extreme personal humility. They will create superb results but shun public praise, and are never boastful. An example of such a leader who epitomized humility is David Packard, the co-founder of Hewlett-Packard, who, in Jim Collins' words, defined himself as a HP man first and a CEO second. Shunning all manner of publicity, Packard is quoted as saying, "You shouldn't gloat about anything you've done; you ought to keep going and find something better to do."

We often confuse humility with timidity. Humility is not cloaking ourselves in an attitude of self-effacement. Humility is all about maintaining our pride about who we are, about our achievements, about our worth – but without arrogance. It's about a quiet confidence without the need to sell our wares.

A friend once asked Samuel B Morse, the inventor of the telegraph, "Professor, while you were at your experiments, did you ever come to a stage when you did not know what to do next?" "Oh yes, more than once," answered Morse. "And at such times, what did you do next?" "I must answer you in confidence," replied the inventor modestly, "but it is a matter of which the public knows nothing. Whenever I could not see my way clearly, I knelt down and prayed to God for light and understanding."

"And did the light and understanding come?" asked the friend. "Yes," declared Morse, "and may I tell you that when flattering honours came to me from America and Europe on Account of my invention which bears my name, I never felt I deserved them. I had made a valuable application of electricity, not because I was superior to other men, but solely because God, who meant it for mankind, must reveal it to someone, and was pleased to reveal it to me."

Humility is not an attitude or a manner of etiquette; true humility is a way of life, an aspect of our temperament. Humility cannot be taught, it must be imbibed, inculcated through self-awareness.

A big 'Physical Culture Conference' was held, some years ago, near Ahmednagar. Gurudev Sadhu Vaswani was invited to speak at the Conference. He asked to be excused. One of the organizers of the Conference came and met me. He brought a word of request from the then Health Minister and added, "Many are anxious to hear him. Thousands of people will gather at the Conference and he must not disappoint us."

I felt tempted. I spoke to Gurudev Sadhu Vaswani. What was his answer? "Let the cobbler cobble his shoes." he said. His words should have moved me to tears. But, I was blind. And I pressed the point. "Thousands of people," I said to him, "will hear you at the Conference. Many of them are anxious to listen to you. Why must you disappoint them?"

He smiled a sad smile as though to say, "Alas! For you who are still immersed in the maya, the illusion, of numbers;" with the word of mouth, he said "Keep your throngs and your thousands to yourself! Give me the simple, humble tasks of life!" He taught by precept and example, what it is to walk, pilgrim-like, the 'little way'. His life rings with the message: "Pilgrims are ye all! Walk ye the little way!" Grow in the awareness that your real worth lies not in your outer, empirical self, but your inner imperishable self. The inner self cares little for applause and admiration of others.

Chapter 18
This too shall pass away!

The winds continued to whistle as the rain came smattering down against the window pane. The typhoon was raging outside as a family remained safe in the shelter of their home. A little girl lay in her bed afraid of the rolling roar of the thunder. She closed her eyes tightly and prayed to God. She slowly felt the reassurance of her mother's arms around her, "Don't worry, it's just a storm. It will soon pass." "But mummy, why does God make storms?" she asked. The mother replied softly, "To make us appreciate the sunny days."

Friends, many times, we too are faced with storms, difficulties and depressing times in our lives. And we allow ourselves to be carried away by these storms. We forget that the storm will surely pass and give way to yet another bright, sunny day.

We live in a world in which nothing abides forever. Nothing abides because life is a movement in waves, waves come and waves go. Everything comes to pass. These problems that come to us, the difficulties that we find in our way, the obstacles that are set up on our path they will all pass away. If only you remember this teaching, this too shall pass away, whenever you are surrounded by a problem, you will see what strength and courage you get to face that problem.

Is not our life like a river? It flows on and on, and as it flows, it sometimes cuts through green and beautiful landscapes, sometimes through arid, wild, lonely tracts. When it passes through cool, green woods, it does not say, "How beautiful it is here! I shall stop by, and enjoy this scene a little longer!" It flows on.

When it has to pass through dreary tracts, it does not say, "I refuse to flow through these parts!" It goes on. Like the river, we too, must go on, seeking all the time, the Sea of Life that is God himself.

An old Persian king was wondering what he could give to his son as a present for his sixteenth birthday. He decided on a ring.

When his birthday came, his son, the prince, was very proud of the ring, until he saw what was written on it. For the Persian letters on the ring said, "Even this shall pass away."

The Prince did not understand what those words meant, but he wore the ring and often read the inscription on it. He read it over and over until he knew the words by heart.

Later, he went off to war to fight beside his father. He was struck by an arrow and lay in bed for weeks in great pain. Many times during his illness he would look at the ring and say to himself, "Even this, even this pain, will pass away." And it did. He grew older and got married. He was very happy then, but he kept looking at the ring and saying, "Even this joy will pass away." And it did.

He was crowned king after the death of his father. On his coronation day he looked in a mirror and said to himself, "Even this, even this body of mine will pass away." And it did.

His last words before he died were, "Even this, even this great empire which I rule will pass away." And it did.

Get into the habit of repeating to yourself the words on the ring, "Even this will pass away." You may be sad about something but your sorrow shall turn into joy.

You may be going through something that is hard to bear, remember, "Even this will pass away." You may be elated and excited about something but it shall soon pass away.

If you are tempted to be conceited about something, even that will pass away. What is not eternal does not matter.

There is an inscription over the doorway of the Cathedral Milan, in Italy, which is very much the same as the words on the ring which the Persian king gave to his son.

Over the main doorway are craved three pictures. On the left are some roses and a ribbon. Underneath is written: "All that pleases will pass away".

On the right are a cross and a ribbon and the words: "All that pains will pass away." In the centre is a triangle and in the triangle are the words: "All that matters is eternal!"

Chapter 19
Love and Laugh

One beautiful evening, as I took my usual walk, I found hundreds of birds singing to their hearts' content. And I said, "Birds were created to sing, and they sing. Man was created to love God, when will he give up chasing shadow shapes and start loving God?"

The man who offers his life, his all, at the Lotus Feet of the Lord, works with peace in his heart. He works as a servant of God and man. He sees that men and women suffer in this world of tragedy and tears; he gives to all the service of love. His work does not take him away from God. His work is God-guided. "Not I, but the Father in me works." he says. In his work there is no hustle, no bustle, no fuss, no noise, no aimless rushing about. In his work there is no unrest but peace — the peace that passeth understanding. In his work is love for all!

Of one such man I read, the other day. He was an elderly disciple of Christ. He lived at a time when, to become a devotee of Christ, was to invite death by torture. He was not afraid. He was a simple peasant who lived by the sweat of his brow. As he tilled the land, he sang within his heart, the Name of his Master. He tilled for the love of Christ. His land yielded abundant grain. He kept a little for himself, sharing the rest with the poor in whom he beheld the radiant face of his Beloved. His house was open to all who needed food and shelter. Many were the pilgrims and wayfarers with whom he shared his simple meals and the love of his brave, beautiful heart.

The Government of his day learns of his deep devotion to Jesus. Soldiers are sent to kill him. They arrive at his village, a little after sunset. They want food and shelter for the night. They are told that in the village is a man who denies hospitality to none. They go to him, not knowing that it is he whom they have come to kill. He meets them with the warmth of love, he serves them, he gives them food to eat. When he asks them the purpose of their visit, he learns that they have come to kill him. He does not reveal to them his identity but asks them to spend the night in his cottage. He attends to their needs, he prepares beds for them, he puts them to sleep.

And then what does he do? He does not escape from the village, he goes out and digs a grave for himself. He is not afraid of death. He is happy as a bride on her wedding day. He is eager to meet the Eternal Bridegroom, the Spouse of the soul. He keeps awake the whole night, communing with his Lord and Master.

As the day dawns, he says to the soldiers, "I am he whom you seek. My head is before you, do your duty!" The soldiers are taken aback. They loathe to take the life of this marvelous man and fain would give him a chance to escape. He says to them, "Fear not, brothers! You have come to lay on my poor, undeserving head, the crown of martyrdom. I die for the love of my Master, Jesus Christ!" As they chop off his head, there are tears in the eyes of the soldiers: but his face is filled with an unearthly light. He is not afraid of death. He smiles in the face of death. When they ask him the secret of his life, he says, "The secret is a simple one. I love and laugh. Each moment I delight in the Lord! I try to translate the teachings of my Master in my daily life, and I have the fullness of joy which no man may take away from me!"

"I love and laugh!" How many of us can speak these words? Do we love all men and birds and animals? It is easy to love our friends: do we love those that bear ill-will towards us? It is easy to love our kith and kin, our dear and near ones, do we love strangers? It is easy to love those that praise us, do we love those that persecute us? It is easy to love those that help us, do we love those that spitefully use us or exploit us to selfish ends? It is easy to love those that are rich and wealthy, do we love the poor, the lowly and the lost, the forsaken and forlorn? It is easy to love the 'good' and 'virtuous'; do we love the sinner, the criminal, the thief and the robber? Do we love those that have gone astray and those whom our laws have made prisoners? Do we love birds and animals who, alas, each day are driven to the slaughter house to satisfy our corpulence and edacity? Do we love trees and plants, leaves and flowers and blades of grass? Do we love rivers and seas, hills and mountains, stones and stars? Do we love every grain of sand, every drop of water, every ray of light? Do we love God and all that God has created?

And do we laugh — in all conditions and circumstances of life? It is easy to laugh when fortune favours us, do we laugh when misfortune dogs our footsteps? Do we laugh in the face of suffering and sorrow, of danger and difficulty, of trial and tribulation, of disease and death? Do we laugh when our dear ones desert us, when our friends forsake us? Do we laugh when all around is darkness and not a single star doth shine?

Until we have learnt to love and laugh, we are not ready to be led into the Kingdom of God. Our hearts are hard; they need to become tender, soft, supple. Our soil is not fertile; it needs to be ploughed with love and laughter. If the ground is hard, the seed will not grow. Prepare the ground! Prepare it with love and laughter!

Chapter 20
Wake Up from your Dream

It was Albert Einstein who said, "Reality is merely an illusion, albeit a very persistent one." Yet we cling to these illusions. Life on earth is a life of involvement. As we do our daily work, we naturally get attached. These attachments are ephemeral; they are like mirage in a desert.

I woke up, this morning, with the following words of a Sufi Saint on my lips: "When the heart weeps for what it has lost, the spirit laughs for what it has found." Not until the heart weeps when our own dear ones misunderstand us, does the spirit awake.

We all are asleep, dreaming the cosmic dream. "You all are asleep," sings Shabistari, "and your vision is a dream. All you are seeing is a mirage." But this realisation comes to us only when we enter into the Great Awakening. "Fools think they are awake now," says the Chinese Philosopher, Chuang-tse. And he describes an amusing experience in the following words. "Once upon a time," he says, "I, Chuang-tse, dreamt I was a butterfly, fluttering hither and thither; to all intents and purposes, a butterfly. I was conscious only of following my fancies as a butterfly, and was unconscious of my individuality as a man. Suddenly, I awoke, and there I lay, myself again. Now, I do not know whether I am now a butterfly dreaming or I am a man."

I had a similar dream once which left a deep impression on me. I dreamt that four thieves had broken into a rich friend's house and were caught red-handed. They appeared to be very poor, and to me it was obvious that poverty had driven them to commit theft. They were being handed over to the police when I pleaded with my friend to have mercy on the poor souls and let them off, not without first giving them a good, hearty meal. As I was dreaming thus, it appears that four thieves 'actually' broke into the compound of our building and were caught red-handed. And my friends came to wake me up, saying, "We have caught four thieves. We want your consent to hand them over to the police." Half awake, I said, "Shall I give you my consent to hand over the four thieves to the police or shall I continue to plead with my friend to let off the four thieves?"

Yes, we all are asleep, dreaming the cosmic dream. Therefore let us not regard anything as real. Let us not seek our happiness in objects and persons who only appear to be real, as things and men in a dream appear to be real while we are dreaming. If we do so, we will be a laughing-stock to those that are awake. I remember how once, as a child, I dreamt that I had a beautiful toy. I was playing with it, when one of my school-mates came and took it away. I cried out loudly, "You dare not take it, it is mine." And I awoke! My mother and sisters and brothers laughed at me, as they asked, "What are you dreaming of?"

When I say 'This is mine, that is mine.' I am; in truth; dreaming. For, in reality, nothing belongs to me. My own body does not belong to me. It was the Buddha who said, "The fool thinks, these sons are mine, these things are mine. When he does not belong to himself, how can anything belong to him?"

The truth is that nothing, no one, belongs to you, and you belong to none. Imagine a spider has woven its own web happily. And when it has woven it so beautifully, it finds that it has become a prisoner of it and cannot escape out of it. That is what we are doing. We are working hard day and night; chasing shadow-shapes, seeking wealth and possessions, we are weaving our own net and ultimately when we get all that we are running after, we find how much a prisoner we are of these things. They have possessed us. Then we find it difficult to get out of that net.

How may we get over the feeling that our dear ones whom we love are ours? The answer is given us by the Sage Yagnavalkya, in the Upanishad. "Let the wife be dear to her husband," he says, "not for the sake of the wife, but for the sake of the *Atman*. And let the son be dear to his mother, not for the sake of the son, but for the sake of the *Atman*." When our relationships are rooted in the truth of the *Atman*, then we shall be free from attachment, and we shall love each other as free souls. Such love will be pure and unselfish and, in certain cases, more intense than that of a husband for his wife. Such love will liberate us from bondage to earthly objects and creatures.

We need to awaken from this dream-like world, with its profits and losses, its pleasure and pain, and prepare to look for our true home which is within us.

Chapter 21
Quieten the Mind

E ach one of us carries around with ourselves an extremely sharp instrument which causes chaos in our lives and plays havoc with our emotions. We have no idea how to control it. It did not come with an instruction manual or a training guide. You may have guessed what it is. It is our mind.

A holy man moves out on a dark night, carrying a lantern in one of his hands and a small bundle containing clothes and books in the other. He feels so blissful, so carefree; he regards himself as one of the happiest of men on earth. As he moves on, he hears a sound of an approaching motor cycle. The motor cycle is speeding fast. But the motor cycle is without a light. And this holy man says to himself, this motor cyclist is moving out on a dark night without a light, maybe he will meet with an accident, let me pass on my lantern to him. It will be useful to him. He signals to the motor cyclist to stop. But the motor cyclist does not stop. He rushes past, almost dropping the holy man down. And the holy man cries out, "O my brother, wait and take this lantern from me, for I am afraid on this dark night without a light you may meet with an accident, and may be you kill someone or injure yourself." And the motor cyclist shouts back, "I cannot stop, I have no breaks."

Is this not the predicament of the modern man? The modern man is also speeding fast. He has no breaks. He cannot stop. He has no light. He is passing through the darkness of a starless night. Modern civilisation offers us so many comforts and conveniences, but in spite of them all, life seems to be dark and dull, life seems to have lost its meaning.

This story my friends is a parable and the motorcycle represents the body of man. The engine of the motorcycle represents the mind of man. The engine is driving fast, our mind is moving at a very fast rate. All the time it is wandering, wandering,

wandering and even as it wanders we wander with the mind. We have wandered for years together, we have achieved nothing. Like a rolling stone we have gathered no moss. It is time for us to stop. It is time for us to take account of things. We have wandered so much, we have wandered so long, I do not know how long yet remains to us. In the time that is yet left to us, let us awaken, let us open our eyes. The light of the motorcycle represents self-knowledge and the breaks of the motorcycle represent self-discipline. These are two things that modern man needs. He needs self-discipline on the one hand, and he needs self knowledge on the other. Self-discipline, for it has been said that he who has learnt to conquer himself, is greater than he who has conquered the whole world.

The mind wanders among objects as a monkey does from tree to tree. In a recent study published in the West, scientists have discovered that over half our thoughts at any given time, are NOT really related to what we are doing at that moment! Surprisingly, we tend to be elsewhere even for casual and presumably enjoyable activities, like watching TV or having a conversation. While you might hope all this mental wandering is taking us to happier places, the data say otherwise. Just like the wise traditions teach, we are happiest when thought and action are aligned, even if they're only aligned to wash dishes. A person who is ironing a shirt and thinking about ironing is happier than a person who is ironing and thinking about a sunny getaway, the research reports. This pattern holds for every single activity measured in the study. The particular way you spend your day doesn't tell much about how happy you are. Mental presence - the matching of thought to action - is a much better predictor of happiness.

The researchers summarise their work very simply: "A human mind is a wandering mind, and a wandering mind is an unhappy mind."

Friends, it is in the nature of the mind to be restless. It is in the nature of the mind to wander; but it is within our purview to control it. You can try a little exercise. Every time you become aware that the mind wanders, quietly, gently, lovingly, sweetly bring it back to the Divine Presence. Speak to the mind, cajole the mind, treat the mind like a child. Say to the mind, "Mind, how long will you wander? So many years of this life you have wandered, and you have wandered birth after birth, through ages, through centuries, through eons, you have wandered, what have you gathered, nothing. Why don't you come and sit with me at the Lotus-feet of the Lord? Let us both sit together in the Divine presence, you will also be happy, I will also be happy and that is all that we need."

He is truly happy who has broken the thralldom of the mind, truly happy, because he is truly free. The mind of such a one becomes his friend, a co-partner in the constructive, creative tasks of life.

Chapter 22
Let God Take Over

When we come into this world, most of us face circumstances similar to Arjuna on the battlefield of Kurukshetra. His plight was pathetic when he was confronted with the fact that he had to fight against his kith and kin.

A feeling of total dejection overpowered his normal reasoning. It was then that Lord Sri Krishna took him through the sea of knowledge that we know as the Bhagavad Gita. After explaining the various paths to self-realisation, Sri Krishna says to Arjuna, "Let me pass on to you a secret of spiritual life." The secret is this, 'Sarvadharman Paritajya

Mamekam Sharnam Virja Renouncing all rites and writ duties come unto me for single refuge, and I shall liberate you from all bondage to sin and suffering, of this have no doubt.' When we surrender ourselves at the feet of the Lord, our sins are all washed away, and our life is transformed by His Divine grace.

As Beloved Sadhu Vaswani puts it:

"The log doth not move; but the river can carry it to the other shore. Let but the log surrender itself to the river that flows. Krishna is the River that flows. Let but a man - no matter how burdened with sins - surrender himself to Him, and He will carry the devotee to the Other Shore!"

There is a story of the little girl who went with her father to climb a mountain. At first, she wished to climb on her own. She said to her father, "Let me do it alone!"

The father let her do it. She moved in front, and the father followed. She was glad to show to her father how strong and capable she was. In due course, the mountain grew steeper and more difficult to climb, she slipped and fell.

The thorns pricked her feet and legs. Tears trickled down her cheeks. She would not give up. She had a strong will and was determined to show her father that she could do it all on her own. At last, the task became too difficult for her and after the most cruel fall of all, she turned weeping to her father. He took her tenderly in his arms and reached her to the peak of the mountain.

When we surrender ourselves, we are taken up in the everlasting Arms of God. And then we know that there is One who is taking care of us. He is Omnipresent, He is Omnipotent, He is Omniscient. He looks after me. My true security is at His Lotus Feet.

When we surrender ourselves to him, he becomes the Captain, who assumes responsibility for our well-being and takes charge of our spiritual progress. He who hath surrendered himself hath found the greatest security of life. All his cares and burdens are borne by the Lord Himself.

What is complete surrender? To surrender ourselves to Him is to accept His Will. We are not yet prepared to do so. We still want our wills to be done.

Our prayers in effect are something like this: "O Lord who art All-powerful! listen to my cry. Rush to my rescue and grant me all that I ask. I want health and happiness. I want bungalows and a beautiful wife. I want wealth and all that wealth can purchase. I want honours and fame. I want a position of power and authority. I want men to dance attendance upon me. I want my name to appear in the papers if not every day, at least, once a week. In short, Lord! I want my will to be done by Thee, and by everyone else!"

To seek refuge is to trust the Lord - fully, completely, entirely. It is to know that He is the one Light that we need in the darkest hours of our life. He is the all-loving, One whose ears are ever attentive to the prayers of His wayward children. He is the all-knowing, One who does the very best for us.

With Him, all things are possible; and if He chooses not to do certain things for us which we want Him to do, it is not because He cannot do them, but because He knows better - he knows we require something else for our own good. So it is that he who has taken refuge in the Lord is ever at peace. "Not my will, but Thy will be done, O Lord." he prays.

Whatever happens, "I accept! I accept! I accept!" is his mantra.

The way of surrender is the way of spiritual conquest, and leads to lasting peace and joy. No life is more secure than a life surrendered to God.

Chapter 23
Explore the Interior World!

E merson, one of the great sages of America, said on one occasion, "What lies before me and what lies behind me are small matters compared to what lies within me." It is the within that needs to be explored. Today we are going crazy exploring outer space. It is true that outer space is infinite. But there is the inner space which needs to be explored. And if only you explore that inner space, you will be amazed. Within you is an infinity of consciousness. If only you will explore it you will be able to pick up pearls and rubies and diamonds.

In our constant state of superficial existence, we continue to ignore the world within. In our persistent chase after shadow-shapes and worldly wealth, we lose sight of our inner consciousness. We emphasise speech, action and outward show; we forget that there is a far more valuable aspect to life called reflection, contemplation, introspection. We have no time to think of the world within! It is within us, that we will find the peace and joy we seek so desperately!

Even as there is an expanding universe outside of us, there is a larger and more wonderful universe within us of which we are not aware. Each one of us has this beauty within us. All we need to do is go within. Most of us, 99% of people die without being aware of the beauty within us.

One day, as the sun was setting, a friend visited the great Sufi woman saint Rabia. He called out to her to come out and see the glamour of colors - oranges, pearly pinks, vibrant purples, in the skies outside. Rabia said to him, "My brother, comes inside. Let me take you inside yourself and you will be deeply amazed at the wonderful colors and sights that you have inside you."

Once man realises this, that all that he wants and all that he needs is within him, he will not have to wander outside.

There came to Gurudev Sadhu Vaswani, one day, a man, travel-weary and tired. In his quest of the unknown, he had visited many places, and met many holy men. He had wandered to many pilgrim-spots, but his quest remained unfulfilled. And he said to Gurudev Sadhu Vaswani, "Much have I wandered and many places of pilgrimage have I visited, but I have not found him yet. Whither may I go?"

Gurudev Sadhu Vaswani said to him, "Brother beloved! He whom thou dost seek, He is not far from thee! He is the deepest self of what thou art. Enter into thyself and know that in thee is He whom thou dost seek. Thou mayst wander the wide world through, thou will not find Him outside thee, for He is within! And in all thy search never forget that the one thou seekest is He who seeketh thee!"

To grow in the inner life, the life of the spirit, we need to withdraw from the outer world of noise and excitement. Therefore, we stress on the practice of silence everyday. Each day, we must spend some time; at least an hour; in silence. At the very start, perhaps, it will be difficult to sit in silence for an hour in a stretch. Then it would be well if we practice silence for about a quarter of an hour, four times a day.

In due course, the mind will become calm and clear as the surface of a lake on a windless day. Such a mind will become a source of in describable joy and peace. Significant are the words of the Upanishad, "The mind alone is the cause of man's bondage; the mind is, also an instrument of man's liberation."

Everyday preferably at the same time, at the same place go and sit in silence, pray, meditate, do your spiritual thinking. When you are alone meditating with God, no one should disturb you, even urgent messages must wait and the telephone bell must not tinkle. Sitting in silence, if you like, you can take up a name of God, a name which to you is symbolic of God. Or sitting in silence you can pick up a great thought of a great one, revolving in your mind, you will find a chain of thoughts arising out of that one single thought and as you keep on thinking on this one single thought you will sink deeper and deeper within yourselves and you will be blessed with wonderful experiences, interior experiences.

Or sitting in silence, you can pick up an incident from the life of your Guru or a form of God. Say to yourself he was so forgiving when shall I be likewise? He was so patient when shall I be likewise? He was so loving, when shall I be likewise? Choose anything that you like, but every day you must sit in silence and do your spiritual thinking.

Silence does two good things to us. The first is silence purifies us and the second is silence energies us. Silence strengthens us. As we enter deeper and deeper into silence, we are purified, we are cleansed.

Let us practise silence everyday and, sinking deeper and deeper within, behold the imprisoned splendour.

God built this world in beauty, and we were meant to live our lives in the fullness of freedom and joy. Man was meant to live like a song-bird, unfettered, free. Alas, man finds himself cribbed, cabined, confined. He has become like a bird in a cage – he is trapped in the cage of self-centeredness!

Not until self-centeredness goes may man become truly happy and free; and the prison of self-centeredness opens with the key of humility. Especially important for the seeker on the path is humility; for it sets free the swan bird of the soul, and the soul can soar into radiance and joy!

My friends, within every one of us there are two selves. There is the lower self with which we are familiar. It is what we call the ego self. It is the self of passion and pride. It is the self of lust and hatred and greed. It is the self of selfishness and miserliness. We have identified ourselves with this lower self. Actually this lower self, this ego self is such a tiny thing. It is a speck of a speck of a speck. But because we have identified ourselves with it, we magnify it beyond all proportions in our daily life. This ego self sits on the threshold of our consciousness and easily catches us, captures us, misleads us, leads us astray.

But there is the larger self, the nobler self, the true self, in the words of the Bhagavad Gita the Self Supreme. We are unaware of the existence of this self. But in the measure in which we identify ourselves with this larger self, this supreme self, in that measure the divine power, the potential that lies hidden within us will be unfolded and we will find wonderful things happening in our daily life.

We are caught in the web of the ego, the lower self, but are not even willing to give it up. The ego is a thief; the ego is our most dangerous enemy; it is the force that separates the Soul from God. It is the impenetrable wall which hides us from the Light with dark shadows of 'I', 'Me' and 'Mine' falling on us, obstructing our vision. The ego is subtle; its workings are not obvious. As the seeker is making progress on the path, he may pride himself on his efforts. Sometimes he thinks he is close to success. Sometimes he feels he has attained his goal. Sometimes he realises with despair, that it is very difficult to be spiritual. Then comes to him the realisation that his efforts and endeavours are not pure, but tainted, spotted. The darkest spot of them all, he realises, is the ego – the lower self – the 'I'. And then he begins to realise that he must transcend the ego to enter into the Limitless. He begins to realise that of his own accord, he can do nothing, achieve nothing. He learns to accept all that comes to him – abasement, criticism, disappointments – as the Will of God. As the love of God and Guru fills him, egoism dies. When you conquer the ego and seek the lowest place, the grace of God will flood into your life, and not only will you be truly blessed, but you will also be a source of blessing to many.

A man of God was once asked, "What is the way to God?"

He replied, "When thou hast vanished on

the way then thou hast come to God!"

So the disciple too, must 'vanish' so that he may become the seeker who is prepared to see the Light!

Trample under your feet your sense of I-ness. Grind it to powder and eat it at every meal – breakfast, lunch, dinner! The more you forget yourself, the more you will get closer to God!

Annihilate your ego. Become nothing. Not even zero. For zero too has space in it. There are two zeroes I am familiar with, in two different numeral scripts. The English zero is written like an O and the Sindhi zero is written simply as a dot. My beloved Master Sadhu Vaswani urged us to become the Sindhi zero, a dot, a nothing. Once your ego is annihilated you would see His image in all; you would acknowledge His presence in everything around you, birds, animals, trees, plants, fruits, flowers and human beings - experience this awareness. Start now, for the time is short and the journey is long. Annihilate yourself. And behold the vision of Lord!

Yogi Mahadev did not have any disciple.

One day, a young man approached him and begged him to accept him as his disciple. To this the yogi said, "I will accept you as my disciple on one condition. Go to the peak of the mountain and jump from there." The young man was stunned. He said, "If I jump from the peak of the mountain I shall die." The yogi smiled at him and said, "Unless and until you die, how would you be re-born?" The young man pleaded, "Please explain." The yogi replied, "To understand this you will have to go to a farmer. He will explain it to you. It is only when the seeds are totally buried that the new crop comes up. Until the grains of wheat die in the earth, they cannot yield a new crop."

Remember, you are like a seed. The periphery is finite, but deep within you are infinite possibilities. Just as a seed needs to give up its seed-hood to grow into a plant, unless we are ready to lose ourselves completely we cannot grow anew. The art of wise living is the art of dying.

One of the most basic concepts of economics is want vs. need. A need is something you have to have, something you can't do without like air. A want is something you would like to have. It is not absolutely necessary, but it would be a good thing to have. A good example is jewellery.

So many of us are satisfied with what the world gives and the world takes away. So many of us are satisfied with the possessions and belongings, the pleasures and the power of this earth. We have no need for God. Living amidst the luxuries of life, we do not feel the need for the Lord, until we realise that this world cannot give us what we truly require. Then the feeling of uneasiness stirs. The troubled spirit begins to feel the longing for liberation.

Fortunate is the one whose heart longs for the love of the Lord. Such a devotee is rare, for he realises that these luxuries of life are trinkets and the joy they give is ephemeral and superficial. Within his heart is a wound festered by separation from the Beloved. Such a devotee cries out, even as he sits in meditation, "O Lord, where should I search for You? Where will I find You? I need Thee, and only Thee. I need nothing else besides." We must create this need for God. And when this need occurs, then it is that the Lord comes and blesses us.

We shed tears for the things which the world gives and the world takes away. We weep for our dear and near ones, who belong to a world of transience. In this world nothing abides! Everything, every form, is as a bubble floating on the surface of water. One moment it is: another moment it has vanished! Alone God is! And Blessed is the person whose heart is filled with pure love and longing for the Eternal Lord. A mark of this love is tears. When your eyes shed tears for the love of God, He is not from you afar. Just as the reddening of the skies at dawn is a sure sign that the sun is about to rise, even so the reddening of the eyes by tears of pure love and longing for His vision is a sure sign that the Lord will soon appear to you. For tears cleanse the stained mirror of the heart and enable you to behold the Beauteous Face of the Beloved therein!

Let us awaken an aspiration in our hearts. We read, do we not, that Sri Krishna played tricks with the Gopis, enticed them in his love and then disappeared, leaving the Gopis yearning for him. I hardly need to tell you that this story of Krishna Leela, actually symbolises the highest aspiration that any human soul can have – that is, the yearning of the *jivatma* (individual soul) for the *paramatma* (the Supreme Being). In the same way, you must kindle a longing for Him in your heart.

There was a seeker, a disciple, he came to his Guru, and said to him, "Master, tell me when is it that I will have a vision of God?" The master did not give an answer but after a little while took his disciple to the river for a bath. When both of them were in the middle of waters, the master caught hold of the disciple by his neck and immersed him deep in the waters. The poor disciple struggled to lift up his face, but the master was a stronger man. And the disciple could not match his strength against him. After a little while the master let the disciple go and he took his head out of the waters. And the master asked him, "Tell me my child, what was your feeling when your head, when your face was immersed in the waters?" And the disciple said, "Master I forgot everything. I did not remember anything. I only longed for a breath of air so that I might continue to live. I thought I was dying." And the master said to him, "When you feel likewise for God, when such a need wakes up in your heart for God then remember, it is the time that you will have the vision of God."

Long for God, said that great saint of India, Sri Ramakrishna Paramhansa, long for God even as a miser longs for gold. Long for God even as a lover longs for his beloved, all the time he is thinking of his beloved. Long for God even as a child longs for his mother whom he has lost somewhere. When you have that longing, keep on telling God again and again, "God I need you, I don't want anything else." It is true you may want other things, but start with that, make a start and say I don't want anything else.

Gradually your mind will come into that frame and you will truly not want anything except God. And once God comes to know that you need Him and nothing besides Him, He will come and reveal Himself to you. God is the source of love, joy and peace, the source of anything that you may need and you will lack nothing.

God is more real than all these things that we perceive with our outer senses. You can hear God speak to you, you can see the face of God. But to be able to see God, labour is needed and that labour is intense yearning of the heart, deep longing of the heart. Let that yearning rise and take you on a higher elevation above the mundane acts of daily living. The heart wrenching soulful cry for the Beloved will put you on the spiritual path. You will find He is by you, guarding you and guiding you at every step of your life.

Chapter 26
Be Rooted in Love

It was about nine o'clock in the night. A few of us sat together, we were all kindred souls. We spoke to each other gently, softly, even as the moon-beams speak to lilies in a lake. And then something happened.

Over a slight matter there was a difference of opinion. It led to a hot discussion between me and one whom I hold in high esteem. The pitch of our voices kept on rising. I felt, I was right; he felt, he was right. Out of a conflict of right with right cometh tragedy. And after some minutes of wordy exchange, as we took leave of each other, my friend felt miserable and I felt unhappy.

Just then someone spoke to me with the simple frankness of a happy child.

And though she spoke out of the tenderness of her heart, every word she uttered was a whip. "You write such beautiful things" she said to me, "and in your conversation with friends and others you give expression to such wondrous things of the Spirit. How often have you not urged that compassion is the secret of true life? And yet, as you spoke now to a brother, you became loveless! The tone of your voice was as the hissing of a snake and your words burnt as live coal!"

"How true." I said to myself. And in sheer shame, I hung low my head.

In silence I asked myself, "Why did I use harsh words? Why?" And the answer came, "Because my life is not yet rooted in love. The roots of my life are elsewhere. Let me take care of my roots. Life is the root, words are as flowers and action is the fruit. If we are not rooted in love, our words go wild and our work more often than not becomes a curse."

That night I kept awake. I sat in my quiet room, shedding unbidden tears of repentance. And then, methinks, I heard a voice say:

"My child, weep not, nor be disheartened. But pray for light and for strength to walk whither the light may lead!" And I said, "You know the burden that sits heavy on my heart. Tell me what I may do?"

And the Voice said, "My child, Let silence be the law of your life; for silence hurts no one. And when you feel like breaking your silence, ask yourself if what you have to say is something better than silence. If so, say it, else remain silent."

I felt like asking a question. But before I opened my lips, I said to myself, "Surely, my question is not better than silence, so let me be silent!"

The Voice continued, "If only we could collect the words each one of us speaks, what a huge mountain they would make! Himalayas of words have passed through these tiny lips. And all these words, as it seems to me, come under five categories:

1. Words inspired by love of God. These are the words we utter in adoration of the Eternal - the cry of the soul to the Over soul, the songs sung in praise of the Most High, prayer, *kirtan* and *jap* of the Sacred Name.

2. Words inspired by love of fellow-men. These are the words of comfort and consolation we pass on to those who suffer and struggle and are in sorrow-words which cheer them on life's lonesome way.

3. Words which wound and hurt and kill. These are the words inspired by jealousy, envy, anger, malice or hatred. How often do we not speak ill of others, little knowing what havoc we cause! An archer shoots to kill. More dangerous is the man with a forked tongue. Every time he opens his lips, he sends forth shafts which strike and sting.

4. Words inspired by self-love. These are the words prompted by egoism, by greed and sensuality. How often do we not 'brag' about our so-called 'achievements' or speak in self- righteous pride! And see, how happy men feel when they indulge in obscene and sensual talk! And when it comes to making a little material gain, men alas! have no hesitation in speaking an untruth. They gain a little and lose their all.

5. Idle words. These are the words men utter without rhyme or reason, merely to while

away their time. The conversations of men are filled with silly questions and imbecile answers, which make our homes centers of idle gossip and our clubs and meeting-places so many towers of Babel. Against this type of talk did Jesus warn, when he said, "But I say unto you, that every idle word that men shall speak, they shall give an account thereof, in the day of judgement."

I listened in rapt attention. And the Voice continued: "When you purchase an earthen-vessel, you strike it and from the sound make out if it is cracked or not. So, too, is the integrity of man proved by his speech. If the words a man utters belong to the first two classes, verily, is he blessed among mortals. Such an one spreads sunshine wherever he goes!"

Chapter 27
Behold the Light

This happened many, many years ago. It was the hour of dusk. Gloom spread over the earth, there was glamour in the skies. I sat at the feet of my beloved Master, Sadhu Vaswani; I put to him this question: Master, what may a man do to be enlightened?

And the Master said: Three things are needed:

1. *Sanga*: to be enlightened, you must be in contact with a man of Light, an Illuminated One. To live with such an one is a rare privilege, his life will give more than a million books can. Out of light cometh light, and a man of Light will wake up within you the centre of light.

2. Meditation: through meditation you will gradually grow into harmony with the man of Light. Meditation aims at harmony, rhythmic vibration. And you will, through meditation, become more and more magnetic. The shouts and shows of modern life produce discord. Never was the world more chaotic than it is today: and never was the need greater than today of magnetic men. Our schools and colleges aim at making the students intellectual. A new culture is needed to make them magnetic. Intellectual youths are often controversial and aggressive; they disintegrate, break up, sunder apart. Magnetic youths are needed to integrate, harmonise and unify.

Remember, too, that you are helped on in meditation by spiritual pictures and symbols.

As you grow in meditation, you will find how veil after veil is withdrawn, until a new revelation of what you are in the depths rises before you; a new consciousness of your hidden powers awakes within you. You become conscious of new reserves of life in your being; you have but to tap them and through you, will flow *shakti*, energy to others.

The man of meditation becomes a centre of force. His very silence is dynamic. He is so unlike a reformer. The magnetic man does not fight, does not denounce. His words are not those of a propagandist or a preacher of a party or creed. His words are sparks of the fire of life. His very silence shines as light, burns as flame!

3. Love, the service of love: Don't aim at big things. Organisations, institutions, imposing associations, let them be. But, my child, you be happy to serve in little things, little acts of kindness, little deeds of love. And, in every act of service, whether done to a bird or animal or a poor, lowly man in need or suffering, what you give is an offering to your Guru, your *Ishta*, the God-man, the man of Light, the Enlightened One. With him you are, one day, blended in wisdom and love. Then every act of your *seva* (service) becomes a song; and you become a flute through which the Lord singeth to bless and heal.

The process of receiving the Divine Light is an ascent from height to height and a descent from depth to depth. Has the process an ending? Through *sanga*, meditation and *seva*, the mirror of the heart is cleansed of impurities. When the heart is pure enough, it focuses rays of the Divine Sun and hears the

Naad, Shabda, the word 'I am', '*Sat Naam*', '*Om Tat sat*', '*Om*', '*Illahu*'!

In different ways is uttered the One Word. And in that Supreme vision of the Heart, world upon world is seen offering homage to God and His *avataras,* God and His saints.

This vision appears, at first, as a flash, then as a series of flashes. The flashes gradually assume definite forms, as you grow in the power of meditation and in purity of the heart. The lamp, the flame, the stars, the moon, the sun, the lotus, the flute and the cross are some of the forms in which the vision gleams. And, sometimes, you are overwhelmed by the Light of the Vision: the Light shines as a hundred suns."

And I asked, "What is the test of this Light?"

The Master said, "A test of this Light is the joy aroused in the heart. This joy, bliss is the *ananda* of which the *Rishis* have sung in rapturous strains.

"Out of *ananda*," we read, "are the worlds born. When this *ananda*, bliss, fills you, you see the One within you and the One around you and the One beyond you and the One in the heart, and the One in this world and the stars, the One in the soul and the One in all - all things, all creatures, all atoms and all *jivas* (living beings).

The bliss which grows out of this vision of the One in all, thrills you to an ecstasy in which there is neither space nor time, neither day nor night, neither far nor near, neither East nor West. The bliss is unspeakable, the bliss passeth understanding. The intellect fades into the night, the words falter. And having beheld the glory, you enter into silence.

In this silence, your mundane knowledge is seen to be ignorance. In this bliss all desires melt away. You see the futility of outer forms - the yellow robe, the saffron turban, the *sanyasin*'s staff, the ascetic's seclusion from men. You see in the outer crafts and creeds and ceremonials the subtleties of the desire-nature. In this Light, your 'self' hath vanished. You have sacrificed yourself to the Eternal Self; you have entered into the Shrine of Silence.

Modern life is stressful. The noise and the frantic pace of the work-a-day world take their toll on the spirit. Everybody knows this, but the sad irony is how poorly people deal with it. They attempt to escape from noise and commotion into more noise and commotion. The empty moments are filled with the artificial noises of electronic entertainment. In the city many escape on weekends to the countryside for vacations, but they take the city with them. In this age of noise, it is imperative for all of us to make efforts to step out of the daily din and clamour and enter into the silence within.

The seventeenth century French philosopher Pascal said, "All man's miseries derive from not being able to sit quietly in a room alone." Within every one of us is a realm of peace, power, perfection. Through practice, we can, at will, enter this realm and contact God. When we do so through meditation, we become conscious of infinite power, a wondrous peace, and realise that everything is perfect and in its own place.

One day we asked Gurudev Sadhu Vaswani, "Master, tell us what is meditation? We hear of it so often, but tell us in a few simple words what meditation is?" And in answer to this question Beloved Gurudev said, "Meditation is withdrawal. Meditation is retreat, meditation is detachment from the outer to know myself. Meditation is turning within."

Meditation, thus, is directing our attention to the Eternal and keeping it there for a while. Some people describe meditation as an art; others call it a science. It would be truer to say that it is a process or technique by which we link ourselves with the highest state of 'awareness' or 'consciousness' that we can reach. To grow in the inner life, the life of the Spirit, we need to withdraw from the outer world of noise and excitement. As we enter deeper and deeper into the silence that is within us, we unfold hidden Shakti, hidden powers of the spirit. We are endowed with a phenomenal dose of energy. We get the strength to triumph over the difficulties and dangers that we encounter. Meditation is like an energy capsule that gives you the vigour required to face life.

In meditation, one can connect with that which is greater than our individual self – our Infinite Source, the Absolute which for want of a better word we call God! When one establishes a link with God, one feels rejuvenated and energised. There is a prevailing sense of positive, calming relaxation. The healing of the body becomes an ongoing automatic process.

Anyone can practice meditation. It's simple and inexpensive, and it doesn't require any special equipment. You can practice meditation wherever you are — whether you're out for a walk, riding the bus, waiting at the doctor's office or even in the middle of a business meeting. All you are required to do is take a short break, pause for a while and withdraw your attention.

In a day and night cycle God gives each one of us 1440 minutes. Out of these 1440 minutes, all we are required to do is to give 10 minutes to re-energising our self. These 10 minutes could be broken into 5 units of 2 minutes each. And these 5 units we can easily remember. The first unit on getting up in the morning, the second unit just before we take breakfast, the third unit just before we take lunch, the fourth unit just before we take dinner and the fifth unit as we are about to slip into sleep. Let us start right now.

Let us take in a deep breath, as we take in the breath, as we inhale let us repeat to ourselves, 'God do please enter into my life'. Let this prayer come out of the very depths of your heart. Let it be filled with all the longing the yearning of which you are capable. And then when you exhale the breath, repeat the words, 'Thank you God for entering my life'. It is as simple as that. As you inhale, 'God do please enter into my life'. As you exhale, 'Thank you God for entering my life'. Doing this 12 times will take you only 2 minutes. Do this 5 times in a day once on getting up in the morning, once before you take breakfast, once before you take lunch, once before you take dinner and once as you are just about to slip into sleep. Sooner or later it will change your life. You will feel drawn to God. You will feel that God is with you all the time. You will become conscious of the presence of God in every little thing that you do. You will feel relaxed and strengthened.

In today's world where stress catches on faster than the eye can see or the mind can perceive, meditation is no more a luxury. It is a necessity. To be unconditionally happy and to have peace of mind, we need to tap into the power of meditation.

Chapter 29
Bask in the Guru's Radiant Presence

In the biting cold of winter, our heart yearns for the warm golden rays of the sun. Similarly, when disheartened by the changing vicissitudes of life, we yearn for the balancing force; we seek a person who would show us a way out. The one who lovingly leads us out of darkness into light, out of coldness into warmth, is the Guru. The Guru is here with this sacred mission: to reveal God's love to us, and to lead our erring, wandering souls back to God.

Caught in the web of maya, caught in the snare of sensual desires and worldly pleasures, we accumulate bad karma, birth after birth after birth. Alas, our poor efforts are not enough to cleanse these impurities. But the Guru's grace can cleanse us and lead us towards the Divine Light of God. The Guru has the magic broom with which he can cleanse away our karmic filth. The Guru is a great cleanser, a great purifier – not merely a great teacher.

A Guru inspires us by his living example. He provides tremendous powers of incentive and inspiration. He cures us of crippling negative emotions. He sees the potential in us that we ourselves are not aware of. Above all, he encourages us to believe that we are also capable of achieving what he has!

As the seeker proceeds on the path, he must never forget that he is always under the umbrella of his Guru. The Guru is the great protector. But it is up to us to make full use of his protection. We need to walk in obedience to the teachings and ideals of the Guru.

The Guru needs nothing else from his disciples, neither riches nor possessions nor power, he needs but this one thing – complete obedience. Doing 8 out of 10 things the Guru wants us to do – is doing them for yourself, for your ego. It is not obeying the Guru. The Guru expects implicit obedience, nothing more, nothing less. A true disciple walks the path of obedience, not the path of freedom.

Several years ago, a sage came to visit Gurudev Sadhu Vaswani. Gurudev Sadhu Vaswani requested him to say a few words of blessings to the *sangat*. The sage truly spoke a few words, but their depth was so intense that they pierced my heart, and I remember them even today. The sage said that there are many forms of *sadhana* or disciplines, through which we can purify and cleanse our *antahkarana*, our inner self, and come closer to the Divine. But the easiest and the surest way is through association with and service of the Guru.

Service of the Guru or Guru-seva is not just attending to humdrum tasks, to menial work allotted by the Guru. Guru-seva is not meant for the personal profit or advantage of the Guru – for he is above such needs and wants. Guru-*seva* is a *tapasya*, an austerity, which the disciple undertakes for his own spiritual growth and benefit. Service of the Guru purifies, cleanses and awakens the heart.

The 'service' that we offer to our parents, friends, family and other loved ones, is service born out of our love and personal motivation to serve them, and be of utmost help to them. In the service of the Guru, there is or should be, no such personal interest. In loving the Guru, meditating upon the Guru's form, in offering our devotion to the Guru and in humbly serving him, we must remember – we are serving God in the form of the Guru. Even when the disciple has attained self-realisation, he will continue to serve God and Guru as before.

When we serve the Guru lovingly, the Guru reaches out to us; and with his grace, annihilates the ego; he tears away the wheels of ignorance which shield us from self-realisation; he reveals our true identity to us – *Tat Twamasi*, That art Thou! It is his grace that liberates us from bondage to the circle of life and death.

Our prayer to the Guru is:
Without you, Beloved Gurudev,
My life is meaningless
Without you, I am directionless and rudderless
With you, I can scale the highest peak
With you, life is never bleak.

There is a manual which mentions 1, 25,000 *sadhanas*, which an aspirant could practice to achieve liberation. But among all, the most effective one is basking in the radiant presence of the Guru and rendering service to him. If ever you get an opportunity to be in the presence of the Guru, do not barter it even if you are offered the entire wealth of the world or its sovereignty. We must be ever alert and constantly aware of every opportunity of being near the Guru, and of rendering service to him, in any way possible.

Chapter 30
A Grain of Grace Sufficeth!

A great saint from the West has said, "What God is by nature, man becomes by grace." For a renewal of life, God's grace is needed. The difficult becomes easy when the grace (*kripa*) of God or a *Satpurukha* descends upon us.

There is a beautiful story I read somewhere concerning an auction at which several articles were sold. The auctioneer picked up an old and damaged violin, and asked if anyone would have it. Finding the instrument in a miserable condition, the people smiled. A voice was heard, "One shilling." The crowd roared and some cried, "Let him have it!" The auctioneer paused for a while, then said, "Perhaps a violinist would like to try it."

An old man took the old violin and, placing it under his chin, played such beautiful melodies that finally the violin was sold for one hundred pounds.

A seemingly worthless thing can become precious in the hands of a master. Many of us feel that we are useless, worth very little or nothing. We surrender ourselves to a great Master and He can reveal our hidden value and, through us, do great things with God's grace.

What is grace? Grace is a gift that the Guru bestows on us unconditionally when he is pleased. Grace is not something that we earn or something that is showered on us for a specific reason. If it were so, it would not be grace. Grace knows no laws, you cannot deserve grace. For example, if you need 35 marks to pass an examination and you have scored only 32 marks, the examiner can have sympathy and give you 3 grace marks. You have not earned those 3 marks, those are grace marks given by the examiner so that you may pass the examination. It is just grace. You do not deserve it.

As we set out on the spiritual path, we stumble and fall many times. But there is an invisible hand that guides us; an effulgent light that shines before us. This is the light of the Guru's grace. He knows well the twists and turns and curves on the path that we can stumble upon. His light will help us realise the truth, remove the obstacles from the path and proceed slowly but steadily towards the destination. The light shines because of his grace; the hand guides us because of his grace.

The Master gives his love and grace to us at every step, as we journey back to our true home. We need only to open our hearts towards him to receive these blessings. For example, the Niagara Falls carry water in abundance, yet the one who comes with a thimble will only receive a few drops. If someone comes with a cup or a bowl, he will get proportionately more. But the one who puts a big bucket under the falls, can draw water abundantly. It is, therefore, not a question of whether the Master's grace is, but how much grace we want.

The Guru is the ocean of grace; he is also the transmitter of grace - but we have to yearn for this grace, we have to allow the Guru to work on us so that we may receive his grace. For the Gurus grace has not only to be bestowed, not only to be given, but it has also to be received. It can be received when we ask for it through our actions - it is not something we need to ask for merely in words. When we make the effort to obey and please our Master, when our spiritual practice becomes our very life, we will experience his grace in abundance.

Gurudev Sadhu Vaswani was once asked, "What must I do to receive His grace?" He answered:

1. I must seek Him every day.

2. I must have no worldly ambitions.

3. I must accept all suffering.

4. I must welcome what comes to me, joy or pain, love or hate.

5. I must realise that I am but a child and so must ever strive to do the Will of God, the Will of the Divine Mother!

6. I must love silence in the midst of the world's noises and strife.

Gradually, he concluded, I shall grow in the presence of God, seeing Him all around, and beyond Him, nothing, only *sunyam*, a void!

Let me tell you, the greatest boon that life

can give us is the grace of the Guru. It awakens the Divine within us; it illumines us from within; it unfolds the process of self-realisation. Rightly has it been said, "A grain of grace sufficeth!" The man, who has surrendered himself to the Guru and lives by his grace, lacks nothing. A mark of him on whom descends the grace of God is an inner calm a holy peace which no danger, no difficulty, no disappointment can destroy.

Chapter 31
Have you made your Decision?

Once upon a time, there was a girl who could do anything in the world she wanted. All she had to do was choose something and focus. So one day she sat down in front of a blank canvas and began to paint. Every stroke was more perfect than the next, slowly and gracefully converging to build a flawless masterpiece. And when she eventually finished painting, she stared proudly at her work and smiled.

It was obvious to the clouds and the stars, who were always watching over her, that she had a gift. She was an artist. And she knew it too. She felt it in every fiber of her being. But a few moments after she finished painting, she got anxious and quickly stood up. Because she realised that while she had the ability to do anything in the world she wanted to do, she was simply spending her time moving paint around on a piece of canvas.

She felt like there was so much more in the world to see and do – so many options. And if she ultimately decided to do something else with her life, then all the time she spent painting would be a waste. So she glanced at her masterpiece one last time, and walked out the door into the moonlight. And as she walked, she thought, and then she walked some more.

While she was walking, she didn't notice the clouds and the stars in the sky who were trying to signal her, because she was preoccupied with an important decision she had to make. She had to choose one thing to do out of all the possibilities in the world. Should she practice medicine? Or design buildings? Or teach children? She was utterly stumped.

Twenty-five years later, the girl began to cry. Because she realised she had been walking for so long, and that over the years she had become so enamoured by everything that she could do – the endless array of possibilities – that she hadn't done anything meaningful at all. And she learned, at last, that life isn't about possibility – anything is possible. Life is about making a decision – deciding to do something that moves you.

So the girl, who was no longer a girl, purchased some canvas and paint from a local craft store, drove to a nearby park, and began to paint. One stroke gracefully led into the next just as it had so many moons ago. And as she smiled, she continued painting through the day and into the night. Because she had finally made a decision. And there was still some time left to revel in the magic that life is all about.

Have you come to a decision yet, have you made your mind up?

Imagine for a moment you are operating totally in your life's *calling*... your *purpose*. How does it feel? Can you see it? Close your eyes and open your inner vision. Taste how it feels to be submerged in what you have been born to do. Can you hear the cheers of your family and friends celebrating your success? Smell the sweet savour of victoriously overcoming all obstacles to achieve this moment in your life. It feels good, doesn't it?

Is this you? Are you living in fullness every day; maximizing your existence and fully contributing to the world? If not, that's okay because it's never too late to start living YOUR life. Now is the time to commit to fulfilling your purpose and operating fully in that thing that you were created to do.

My dear friends, let me share a secret with you. It is only at the very end of the earthly journey when we look back upon our life, do we realise the time that we have wasted in futile pursuits. But as the saying goes, 'It is never too late'. You can begin from now; and prepare for the long, onward, forward journey, that we all have to undertake sooner or later. You can make the end of your story beautiful!